Cache

Cache

CREATING NATURAL ECONOMIES

SPENCER B. BEEBE
Photography by SAM BEEBE

 ecotrust

Printed and bound in the United States

10 9 8 7 6 5 4 3 2 1
Digit on the right indicates the number of this printing

Library of Congress Cataloging-in-Publication Data available.

ISBN — Hardbound: 978-0-9676364-4-3
ISBN — Softbound: 978-0-9676364-5-0
ISBN — Digital edition: 978-0-9676364-6-7

Published by:

ecotrust

721 NW Ninth Avenue, Suite 200
Portland, OR 97209
ecotrust.org

Produced by:

Carpe Diem Books®
carpediembooks.com

Project manager: Ross Eberman
Editor: Gary Miranda
Copyeditor: Jean Andrews
Proofreader: Cher Paul
Indexer: S. Jane Henderson
Design: theBookDesigners, bookdesigners.com
Manufacturing director: Dick Owsiany

The paper used in this book, Harbor 100 80#, is made from 100%
post-consumer pulp and produced locally by Grays Harbor Paper.
The paper is FSC and Green-e certified and manufactured entirely
with renewable energy. The book is printed with zero VOC inks.

TO JANIE

Contents

Foreword

Spencer Beebe is a tree hugger, with a chainsaw.

And a fish lover, with a fly rod.

He believes deeply in the enduring lessons and truths of native cultures.

He's passionate about wild rivers.

And kayaking.

Did I mention he flies his own plane with his dog in the copilot's seat?.

Spencer is old school—Yale and Williams—and yet he never stops looking for new solutions.

He's suspect of orthodoxies and unafraid of contrarian ways. He is both environmentalist and creator of natural economies.

He's a green banker and a founder first of Conservation International, then Ecotrust, Ecotrust Canada, Salmon Nation, and now Ecotrust Australia.

He's a match-maker of small farms and great chefs.

Everyone should have a friend like Spencer, and every ecosystem should have him hovering over its flora and fauna.

For Spencer is a centurion, constantly on guard for this precious planet we all share, and he has devoted his every waking hour to understanding, protecting, and promoting the natural glories of Mother Earth so that her nurturing ways, which have gotten us this far, will be there forever.

As a novice sailor, he and his young wife set off across the Pacific in a home-built ketch and, against great odds, landed on friendly shores. That early adventure is a metaphor for his life, and in this evocative and inspirational book we can all be on deck, testing the winds and hoisting the sails for our common destiny.

His pilgrimage is a journey to be relished and emulated, a commitment to be encouraged and shared, a life to be honored.

Tom Brokaw
Montana, July 2010

Preface

The concept of natural economies, which urbanist Jane Jacobs considers the key to "a more reliable prosperity," is a concept so self-evident to me by now that it's hard to imagine why it took me so long to arrive. One would think that my having done my undergraduate work in economics and my graduate work in forest ecology would have tipped me off that the two fields had more in common. Not so. How I did arrive at the concept—through a long process of false starts, numerous missteps, and occasional successes—is the central thread of the stories that follow. The first stories track my years with The Nature Conservancy and betray an accurately formulaic pattern—we get a call for help, we spring into action, we save the land. From there things get more complicated as the narrative and I range farther afield—to Washington, D.C., and then to the tropical rain forests of Latin America, first as a foot soldier for The Nature Conservancy and later as one of a renegade bunch that broke ranks to start Conservation International—only to come full circle back to Portland and the temperate rain forests of home, where I founded an organization called Ecotrust.

When I started out with The Nature Conservancy in 1974, I was pretty much a dyed-in-the-wool (dyed green, of course) conservationist. Or "preservationist," since the main idea was to save as much untrammeled land as possible from the encroachment of developers. I lived in a self-fulfilling myth of good guy versus bad guy; the white horse was a great one to ride. Some 20 years later, I had founded Ecotrust and was starting up a commercial bank—a slightly different take on "green." In movie lingo, this is known as "character arc"; to some traditional preservationists, it's known as "selling out." To me, however, it's an example of evolution, not unlike the evolution that occurs all around us in the natural world and which I've come to see as the guiding principle for a radical new way of thinking about economic development—and, I might add, about human happiness.

Spencer B. Beebe
Flora, Oregon, June 2010

Introduction

"Cache," from the French cacher *(to hide), suggests something of value that is hidden. The word originally derives from the Latin* coacticare, *which means simply to pack together or collect. In modern Internet lingo, a cache is a form of memory that holds recently accessed and presumably valuable information with the aim of facilitating future access. All of these meanings bear on the purpose of this book: to collect valuable stories that, if not exactly hidden, deserve to be better known and that, when packed together, might help others remember and apply them as prospects for future enterprise and, ultimately, a more reliable prosperity.*

The Artist

Cache also happens to be the name of the painting by James Lavadour that graces the cover. Lavadour, a member of the Confederated Tribes of Umatilla Indians, is an artist whom my wife Janie represents at her PDX Contemporary Art gallery in Portland, Oregon, and a good friend. His paintings fetch a higher price than those of perhaps any living painter in the Northwest today. Jim had no idea I was working on a book called *Cache;* I had no idea he was working on a painting called *Cache.* The coincidence stunned me. When I asked Jim why he had chosen the name, he said that it came only after a long reflective period, and long after the paintings were complete. "Cache," he said, "is a collection of memories of time and space, the evolution of a long iterative process of painting and repainting a large body of work over a long period of time. It's the distillation of information captured by the events of natural properties of paint interacting with canvas and deeper layers of paint."

Jim's power originates from his deep connection to the land on which the Indian side of his family has lived for thousands of years—the high steppe of the Columbia River plateau in the

1

James Lavadour in his studio on the Confederated Tribes of Umatilla Indians Reservation in northeastern Oregon.

rolling foothills of the Blue Mountains in northeastern Oregon. He is not an illustrator. He is self-trained, unburdened by customs of Western art technique. He doesn't stand on a ridgetop and paint what he sees when wildfire sweeps a deep grassy canyon. He doesn't try to copy nature, nor does he intend to improve upon it. He rises at three in the morning and works in the studio with sweeping kinetic motion to the rhythm of Miles Davis. He works on hundreds of canvases at once, slowly, carefully, incrementally—modifying each one continuously over eight to ten years. It is an evolutionary process in which he is trying to capture natural life forces. He uses the full palette of nature and allows the paint to flow, eddy, drip, and accumulate naturally. Lavadour thinks of himself as a medium between the sedimentary and erosional properties of paint and the fundamental forces and landscape of which he is part. At one time, he explained, he was struggling with a way to express water, so he took a walk along the Umatilla River where he lives. He noticed a stick vibrating in the current, stepped slowly into the river, and, holding the stick gently in his hand, absorbed the energy of water against stick. "Aha," he thought, "that's the way water works!" As he says, "We are part of nature. Everything that's out there is in here"—he taps his hand to his body. "The land is the source of all knowledge."

James Lavadour, *Blue Basalt* (2010).

The Urbanist _____

Cache, of course, is also a pun for cash—that is, currency or prosperity—and many of the stories here are intended to serve as examples of how we can move along the road toward what I call reliable prosperity. As the great urbanist Jane Jacobs, my inspiration for the phrase, put it in *The Nature of Economies*, "Working along with natural principles of development, expansion, sustainability, and correction, people can create economies that are more reliably prosperous than those we have now, and that are also more harmonious with the rest of nature." To do this, however, we need to listen to nature with a kind of attention that approximates what James Lavadour does when he paints.

Jane, one of my intellectual heroes, also wrote, "Nature affords foundations for human life and sets its possibilities and limits." We collectively perk, of course, at the mention of possibilities; at the suggestion of limits, not so much. Jacobs, however, sees them as flip sides of the same coin, her point being that "human beings exist wholly within nature as part of the natural order in every respect" and that, therefore, reliable economic systems will be those that imitate natural ecosystems. "My personal biomimicry project," says a character in one of her Socratic dialogues, "is to learn economics from nature."

Jacobs didn't originate this idea, of course, but she seems to have arrived at it on her own, which is fairly remarkable for someone as essentially urban as she was. Jane, whose books include the now-classics *The Death and Life of Great American Cities* (1961), *The Economy of Cities* (1968), and *Cities and the Wealth of Nations* (1984), was mainly interested in cities, not forests, and she is perhaps best known for her application of the above principle to metropolitan neighborhoods in New York and elsewhere. When, at a rather fragile 82, Jane joined me and others on a floating conference down the Middle Fork of the Salmon River in Idaho to discuss the relationship between conservation and development, she was a charmingly good sport and admitted to never having camped out in her life. Her enthusiastic reaction to the wild outdoors was a surprise, but wonderful to see.

From a very early age, Jane told me, she was curious about how things worked. She remembered how at age ten she was exploring this theme in her neighborhood library. Later she wrote about how the ancient practice of sharing become trading. "How did sticks, bones, and fire differentiate into hammers, spears, scrapers, pokers, and torches, then differentiate further into bows, arrowheads, nets, rafts, pigments, trumpets, bags, and so on." And, later: "Why do some cities flourish and others decay? In what ways does discrimination of gender, race, caste, class, religion, social class, or ideology reduce the amount of work and creativity made possible by the full diversity of society's members? And in what ways does this limit their development prospects?"

In her constant search for how things work, Jacobs observed the most minute and seemingly banal detail, yet synthesized and speculated about large-scale patterns and processes over the whole history of human endeavor. Her fundamental search was to understand how development works. She defined development, a word I use constantly in this book, as "qualitative growth." Expansion, a very different but related process, she described as "quantitative growth." Traditional environmentalists talk a good deal about the limits to growth, as if growth is not natural. Clearly there are limited amounts of soil and water, and a limited capacity of the earth's living systems to support growing populations of humans with increasingly materialistic aspirations. Global climate change, as indicated in part by parts per million of CO_2 in the atmosphere, for example, is a direct measure of greenhouse gas emissions exceeding the capacity of earth systems to absorb the carbon from CO_2. But we shouldn't confuse what Jane Jacobs called "quantitative growth" or expansion, with "qualitative growth" or development. There are few things more natural than growth. Natural systems are constantly growing, dying, adapting, changing, and evolving. New species evolve and develop new networks, which themselves create new opportunities to capture or recycle energy and create new webs from which yet more differentiated species evolve. So too with economies.

Toward the end of Jane Jacobs' seventy-plus years of exploring how things work, she began to look at ways in which successful economic development shared the same principles as ecological development or evolution. Her observation that *"human beings exist wholly within nature as part of the natural order in every respect"* (italics mine) is of critical importance. It is the key both to restoring natural systems and to supporting enduring economic development. Jane goes on to say, "This is difficult for many ecologists and economists to accept" and cautions, "Readers unwilling or unable to breach a barrier that they imagine separates humankind and its works from the rest of nature will be unable to hear what this book is saying."

I have come to agree with Jane Jacobs that we can achieve a more reliable prosperity only by grounding our economic system on principles that operate in the rest of the natural world. We don't need to conquer, save, or improve on nature; we need to emulate it. In the most basic sense, we need to *be* it.

Mt. Hood and the Bull Run Watershed
Portland's Water Supply

Jane Jacobs and the author in Portland.

Me _____

As much as I admire Jane Jacobs's lifelong dedication to "the death and life" of cities and share her enthusiasm for the "nature of economies," I'm also aware that we arrived at the intersection of ecology and economy from almost opposite directions and that, as Jane would have been the first to acknowledge, these origins indeed make a difference. As noted above, Jane was an urbanist, a "city girl" in love with the bustle and energy of city life; I come from generations of people who enjoyed the outdoors. My name "Spencer" comes from Spencer Fullerton Baird, the distinguished second secretary of the Smithsonian Institution, married to my great-great-grandfather Henry Jonathan Biddle's sister Mary. Baird was an ornithologist, author, and collector of the plants and animals from around the world that became the foundation of the Smithsonian's collections, what has become known as "the nation's attic." When he heard that populations of a seabird, the great auk, were disappearing from the North Atlantic, he was quick to send an expedition to collect specimens before they disappeared altogether. He helped to create the U.S. Bureau of Fisheries and played a role in starting salmon hatcheries, thinking technology could replace nature and allow continued logging, mining, damming, and irrigating the western rivers while still having abundant salmon for fishermen—precisely the "humans can control nature" ideology that has led to much destruction.

Another distant ancestor, Nicholas Biddle, published the first account of the Lewis and Clark Expedition in 1814, which may have started the family's infatuation with moving west. Great grandfather Biddle studied botany and geology in Heidelberg, Germany, and left Philadelphia for the banks of the Columbia River near Vancouver, Washington, in the late 1880s with a young German wife to hunt, fish, camp, and paint wildflowers at will. My grandfather Spencer Biddle's idea of education at Yale was to win the skeet-shooting competitions, then come home with his keen eye on an proper and disciplined life of hunting and fly fishing from Alaska to Argentina.

Mom following four of her five on a tumultuous early river trip. Three Creek Meadows, Oregon.

My father's side included whalers in Mystic, Connecticut, tea merchants in New York, and my great grandfather General Charles Francis Beebe, who came to Portland, Oregon, in 1880. He established the Beebe Company, jobbers to merchant marine, chandlery, and fisheries equipment to the growing trade of sailing ships coming around Cape Horn to the West Coast and the biggest salmon fishery in the world on the Columbia River. Their big store was in Astoria at the mouth of the Columbia, and the family businesses disappeared with the decline of salmon in the mid-1900s. Mom and dad took my four sisters and me camping in the nearby Cascades at every opportunity while growing up in Portland.

So when people ask why I do what I do, I shrug and say I simply fell off the family log. I spent much of my youth in pursuits that were not what most people would think of as typical. While other boys my age were courting friends, I was courting falcons. From the age of 13 until college, I was practicing falconry. This meant late nights reading ancient Persian treatises on the art and practice of hawking and its modern-day equivalents from

The author, age 13, in a nest of golden eagles along the John Day River, Oregon.

twin brothers John and Frank Craighead, who grew up practicing falconry in Pennsylvania, then came west to do research and conservation work on birds of prey and grizzly bears. As I traveled the outback of Oregon looking for nests of hawks, eagles, and falcons, I would often come to a forest or river or meadow known to have been great nesting habitat in the past, but now denuded by clear-cutting, road building, dams, and expanding agriculture. I learned that two nestling prairie falcons, brother and sister, had completely different personalities. I learned that every muscle and feather on the body of a peregrine falcon is the result of millions of years of evolution that weeded out the successful from the unsuccessful, and that the exquisite nature of these birds was something that deserved total respect. Success raising and hunting with a falcon comes only from deep understanding of the particular habits, natural history, and possibilities of each species and learning to work with the bird at your side as its companion and agent of success. I watched wild falcons and hawks at play in the air, making what clearly looked to me like conscious choices about how to spend their time and

The author, age 16, with Artica, a peregrine falcon taken from the nest in Alberta, Canada.

energy. If a white gyrfalcon sitting on a high cliff surveying the landscape of a high arctic river wasn't "sentient," I wondered what the word could possibly mean. When people asked me how I had "trained" the falcon, I would fall silent in wonder at how any one could be so naive as to think that a 14-year-old could train, rather than be trained by, an eagle or falcon whose perfection was the result of so many millenia of experimentation.

So when Jane Jacobs writes, "Economic development is a matter of using the same universal principles that the rest of nature uses," I'm right there with her. While there are surely powerful ways to use capital, technology, and policy incentives to reduce global greenhouse gases, improve energy security, alleviate poverty, and improve environmental conditions, until humankind more broadly embraces the fundamental nature of our relationships with each other and the environment, a significant shift toward a more "reliable prosperity" will elude us. And when Jane goes on to assert, "The alternative isn't to develop some other way; some other way doesn't exist," I'm right there again to second the motion. In fact, my whole career—from traditional land preservation to advocate for new models of economic, social, and environmental well-being—is but an exclamation point after that final sentence.

Or so it seems to me now. When, in 1987, I decided to leave The Nature Conservancy to test a different approach to conservation, the more telling punctuation might well have been a question mark, or perhaps an ellipsis—those little dots that trail off at the end of a sentence to indicate that it's not sure where it's going next. I've always been one to learn by going. So let's go. . .

PART ONE

1974–1991

1

TWO RIVERS: *Getting My Feet Wet*

Very often major turning points in our lives seem inconsequential at the time and are recognized only in hindsight. This was not the case with the event that occurred in Room 26 of the Tabard Inn in Washington, D.C., on January 26, 1987. "The Tabard Inn" has a Shakespearean ring to it, suggesting—not incorrectly in this instance—high drama. My Tabard Inn, which was a small bohemian house of a hotel with good food and decent prices, had become a sort of home away from home during my years as president of The Nature Conservancy's International Program. At the top of the first set of stairs was Room 26, where, on January 26, I was drafting a letter of resignation that I was fully aware would change my life.

The last thing on my mind even a few months earlier had been leaving The Nature Conservancy. The Conservancy was family, profession, and career. It had given me dream jobs running the Northwest Office in Portland (the six Northwestern states), the Western Regional Office in San Francisco (the 13 Western states), and then developing the International Program in Washington, D.C., from 1980 until 1986, when my friend and graduate school colleague Peter Seligmann finally accepted the move from California to Washington to continue the work, allowing me to live at home in the Northwest. During most of those years,

13

*land conservation—saving the "best of the rest (remaining natural eco-
systems) and last of the least (endangered species habitat)"—was, in
my view, the heart of conservation. I loved the private, entrepreneurial
nature of the Conservancy's game, the freedom I had enjoyed buying
land, recruiting board members, hiring staff, and raising money to do
it. And yet I was writing a letter of resignation that would ultimately
lead to the departure of more than 50 of the Conservancy's International
Program 60-plus staff and five key national board members.*

*The Tabard Inn is also, of course, the name of the inn where Chaucer's
famous circle of storytellers gathered to relate their "Canterbury Tales."
As such it seems an appropriate place to begin these stories. Certainly,
as I labored over the wording of our letter of resignation to The Nature
Conservancy, I traveled back in time to the many places I'd visited in
my commitment to "saving the land." The first of these was the Sandy
River, not far from my native city of Portland, Oregon; the second was
another river—Silver Creek, in Idaho.*

The Sandy River, Oregon

Fresh out of graduate school in the summer of 1974, I was lucky
enough to land a job with The Nature Conservancy's Northwest
Office in Portland, Oregon. An $11,000 annual salary, even
though I had to raise it myself or seek employment elsewhere,
seemed like great good fortune. One of my first tasks was to work
with Ken Margolis, my mentor and boss, and the Diack family to
assemble private lands along the Sandy River, just 20 miles east
of Portland.

I'd known the Diacks since childhood. Every Christmas, they
invited their family friends to the farm to cut Christmas trees, eat
homemade soup, sausage, spaghetti, and hotdogs, and drink hot
buttered rum. In return, everyone planted two or three seedling
cedars, pines, firs, or hemlocks. Some of these seedlings were
exotic to the site and created a curious understory mix of tree
species in an otherwise beautiful native forest along the banks of
the clear winter waters of the Sandy. The Diack Christmas party
was a family tradition I remember from my earliest years.

14

Just 20 miles east of Portland, the Sandy River watershed provides old-growth forest conservation, recreation, and clear drinking water for over one million Portland residents.

Arch Diack was a character; so was his brother Sam. Both were doctors—Arch a general surgeon and Sam an internist—living on Portland Heights. Arch had a spark of ingenuity early on and invented a cardiac resuscitator that produced a sizable investment dividend. In 1941, Sam and Arch acquired 270 acres of land, almost three-quarters of a mile on both sides of the Sandy River. Now, years later, they were giving 160 acres of their Sandy River property to The Nature Conservancy—a gift that came with a challenge. Recognizing that 160 acres does not a wilderness river make, the Diacks wanted the Conservancy to commit to a long-term program of protecting an entire six-mile river corridor between Dodge Park to the south and Oxbow Park to the north. This would be no small feat, but the Diacks understood that the anthropogenic mix of native and exotic species resulting from their annual Christmas party was a subset of the larger Sandy River system: part native, part industrial tree farms, weekend houses, fish hatcheries, and hydroelectric dams. It needed to be better understood—they'd funded an annual program of environmental education and research for students at nearby Reed College—and protected on a larger, watershed scale.

Which is where we came in. Our game plan was to target property that threatened the larger river ecosystem with the kind of subdivisions that had invaded the lower river decades before. First, of course, we had to raise some cash.

Our fundraising strategy involved float trips down the rapids of the Sandy River Gorge to enjoy the unique geology, waterfalls, wildlife, and old-growth forests so close to Portland. Our chief guide and orator as we floated the Sandy River with potential supporters was a neighbor of the Diacks named Tom McAllister. Tom was outdoor editor of the *The Oregon Journal*, one of Portland's leading dailies, and had an encyclopedic knowledge of the natural history of the Pacific Northwest. He seemed to know the history of every tiny town in the farthest corners of remote counties, the names of every fish manager, forester, and birdwatcher, and the former abundance of all populations of odd birds. Thanks in great part to Tom's lore, eloquence, and downright charm, a typical daylong trip with six to ten adventuresome participants resulted in $500 to $5,000 in gifts for the program.

Drifting down the Sandy River.

Tom McAllister, our natural historian, in the old-growth forests of the Sandy River.

Still, this was slow going, and we always kept an eye out for bigger fish.

Portland's biggest fish at the time were Howard and Jean Vollum. Howard and his Navy friend Jack Murdock had built Tektronix, one of the great Oregon business success stories thanks to its pioneering development of the oscilloscope and eventually thousands of electronic components. It was also Oregon's largest employer. The problem was that no one in the philanthropy community knew the Vollums, or even so much as a phone number at which I might try my luck. Howard and Jean Vollum were a quiet, unassuming couple busy raising five sons and building up Tektronix. Though they were generous donors for years, almost all of their gifts were made anonymously. Having exhausted all leads to an introduction through the appropriate high-society channels, I was sitting in my office one day when— in a stroke of either desperation or momentary common sense—I picked up the Portland phone directory and looked up Howard Vollum. There it was, his number, right in the phone book!

Emboldened by our river-rafting successes and buoyed up by ingenuity in tracking down the Vollums, I dialed the number, thinking, *What have you got to lose?* I found out soon enough. After several rings, a gruff deep voice answered, "Hello."

"Mr. Vollum?" I said.

"No, this is *Mrs.* Vollum. Who are you?"

I swallowed a large "Oops!" and went into my spiel: "My name is Spencer Beebe. I'm with The Nature Conservancy—"

"What do you want besides my money?" demanded Mrs. Vollum.

My whole life, my new career, flashed before my eyes. I'd done near-death sky-diving, waterfall kayaking, and sailed a homemade boat in gale force winds across the Pacific from Costa Rica to French Polynesia, but none of these experiences had induced the terror I was experiencing in the face of Jean Vollum's question. I seriously considered simply hanging up the phone and handing in my resignation, but I finally managed to blurt out something like, "Your advice about preserving the Sandy River. Would you like to go on a float trip and see it?"

"No, but my son Danny might. He likes rivers. Here's his number." She gave it to me and hung up.

Oh, my God, I thought as I hung up. I had completely blown it. I'd ignored all the most fundamental rules of fundraising: get a proper, personal introduction from just the right person; don't meet through letters or over the phone but one-on-one in an appropriate setting; look your prospective donor in the eye and ask for an absurd amount of money, then shut up; the next person who talks loses. So listen, listen carefully—to the body language, the subtleties of expression and tone, the very particular sensibilities of the prospective donor.

"Call my son"? You have got to be kidding!

"Hey! You're supposed to listen!" I chided myself. *OK, OK, I'll call Danny!* I thought. And I did.

Sophomore at Oregon State, banjo maker and player, outdoorsman, aspiring pilot, river rafter; 220 lbs., 6' 2", red hair, and big

Danny Vollum.

smile—Danny Vollum was an environmentalist through and through. And his mother was right—"Sure, I like rivers," he said. It didn't take a lot of arm-twisting on my part to conscript him to help raft potential donors down the Sandy River.

Eventually, Danny managed to recruit his parents to join us on a float through the Sandy River Gorge as well. Now, Howard Vollum was an

18

electronic and business genius, but his idea of outdoors was between the front door and his car on the way to the office. He showed up for the wilderness raft trip in an overcoat and wing tips. I mentally adjusted my game plan.

The first quarter mile of the run consisted of a rapid called Pipeline, a lively piece of water that has been known to flip many a raft. But I knew there was a friendly little beach just at the rapid's end. There was a trail to that beach, and not wanting to lose the Vollums before I'd landed them, I suggested that Howard and Jean take the 15-minute walk around Pipeline. I gave them what I thought to be clear directions, but we spent a furtive hour waiting on the beach below wondering where they'd gone. We searched the trail, but they were nowhere to be found. I was sure that I'd figuratively, as well as literally, lost them. About an hour later they both showed up sweaty, red-faced, and exhausted: they'd missed the trail and bushwhacked over a boulder field alongside the river instead of along the gentle but apparently hidden trail.

Horrified, I congratulated them on their perseverance.

"Nice job," Danny said. "That was the hardest part of the trip."

I started to help them into their raft when Jean took me aside and told me Howard was suffering an impending diabetic attack and needed sugar—a candy bar, cookies, anything sweet—without which he would have to be rushed to a hospital. We managed to find the crumbling, wet remnants of a Snickers bar stuck to the bottom of a river bag. Howard accepted it graciously and, soon, gamely revived. We headed downstream.

We had a picnic lunch on a sunny beach where Howard poked his finger down through several layers of wet sand and noted its thermodynamic characteristics. This was infinitely more interesting to him than global threats to biodiversity or even local threats to the Sandy. Through it all, however, he was sportingly gracious, and Jean, for her part, had a great time and was genuinely sympathetic to our mission. In the end, a long and productive relationship with the Vollum family was forged.

It took us four years, but with the help of the Vollums and many others, we successfully completed most of the assembly:

almost 500 acres of critical private land in five parcels along six miles of the Sandy River Gorge. Ken Margolis and I also helped convince the federal Bureau of Land Management to protect a magnificent 400-acre stand of old-growth Douglas fir, and the State of Oregon to create the Sandy Wild & Scenic River, which limited development on additional lands. By the standards of the day, we raised a lot of money—over $130,000 in what was one of the more agonizing accumulations of small bits and pieces of funding imaginable. But it was tangible land that met the essential need to preserve examples of earth's full biodiversity in parks and protected areas one hard-won acre at a time.

While the Sandy River project started with a few hundred acres and the dreams of two family doctors, in later years it grew through public-private partnerships and the leadership of a coalition of nongovernmental organizations and state and federal agencies and eventually encompassed an entire 600,000-acre watershed, a river corridor 40 miles long, from its source on Mt. Hood's glaciers to the Columbia River. In the summers of 2007 and 2008, Portland General Electric removed the 1908 Marmot Dam and then the last dam on the Little Sandy River, making the watershed one of the most intact, wild, and free anywhere so close to a major metropolitan area.

As for me, I had, at least, gotten my feet wet in traditional land preservation.

Silver Creek, Idaho

"This is Jack Hemingway, chair of the Idaho Fish and Game Commission," said the voice on the phone early one morning in 1976. "I need some help."

People were always calling our office in those days, asking us to buy land, and this call was no exception, except that the caller's name was Hemingway.

"The Sun Valley Company," the voice said, "is selling Silver Creek. It's 479 acres and several miles of stream at the headwaters—a world-class spring stream and trout fishery." He went on to explain that if the headwaters parcel was sold to developers, the whole river downstream would be in jeopardy, and the Fish and Game Silver Creek land would be weakened. The cost of buying the land would be a half million dollars. He was confident of getting the project funded from state monies, but it would be a year or two before funds would be appropriated. Could The Nature Conservancy acquire it in the meantime? I told him I'd see what I could do.

Shortly thereafter I flew to Hailey, just south of Sun Valley, one nice spring day. By this time I'd confirmed that Hemingway was indeed Ernest's oldest son, a world-class fisherman ("the only thing I could do better than my father," he told me later) who'd lived for some time in Portland. I'd also learned that Silver Creek was indeed one of the great spring creeks in the West—one that my grandfather Biddle fished many times. Jack had said, "If you fish, bring a fly rod along."

Silver Creek, gin-clear spring water in the high desert of southern Idaho.

Climbing down the stairs from a small commuter plane with a tall aluminum rod case with brass end pieces in hand, I was barely on the ground before the rosy-cheeked, mustached, and hale good fellow Hemingway, without so much as introducing himself, asked: "Is that an E. C. Powell cane rod?" He took the case from my hand and opened it right there on the tarmac.

"Hell!" exclaimed Hemingway. "This is a rare handmade classic! Where did you get this?"

"Well, from my grandfather, Spencer Biddle," I said sheepishly.

He frowned. "When I lived in Portland, I got so god-damned sick of hearing about Spencer Biddle, I just wanted to tell him to go fuck himself!" Then he laughed his great, iconic, welcoming laugh, and off we went to Silver Creek.

So that was my introduction to Jack, a great outdoorsman, fly-fishing aficionado, bird hunter, always happy, enthusiastic, and welcoming bon vivant and general good guy. Also the only GI to parachute over France in World War II with a fly rod in his pack.

From the airport, we followed long, straight, dusty roads past irrigated pastures and alfalfa fields 30 miles south of Sun Valley to an inconspicuous winding road around dry, grassy hillsides, overlooking a wide-open green valley. There below us was one of the classic chalk streams of America: gin-clear water meandering slowly through willows, birch, and cattail marshland between mossy banks, and scattered stands of quaking aspen and cottonwood. A great blue heron rookery in the cottonwoods, a western meadowlark singing from atop a sage bush, a pair of red-tailed hawks soaring high above, mallard and green-winged teal feeding in backwater sloughs, the "ker-er-ip, ker-er-ip, pree pree pree" of western kingbirds, and red-winged and yellow-headed blackbirds singing their gurgling territorial calls. Sullivan Lake was fed by spring water flowing right out of the hillside below us, and enormous rainbow trout were audibly slurping hatching mayflies. The trout were clearly visible, taunting our deepest instincts.

This was "Silver Creek music," something a blind person could enjoy with absolute wonder. A classic spring creek, fed by

Guy Bonnivier, the author, and Jack Hemingway at the Silver Creek preserve headquarters.

deep underground upwelling of water through rich mineral-laden soils from the Big Wood River, itself fed from the melting snows of the Sawtooth Mountains. This was water of alkaline quality, high pH, relatively even temperature and flow throughout the year and thus unusually rich in nutrients—a freshwater fish factory. On warm summer evenings, clouds of hatching midges rose from the smooth waters like campfire smoke. Crystalline waters in the high desert. I was hooked by the magic of the place.

Bill Janss, the Sun Valley Company's owner, was amiable and accommodating and wanted to see Silver Creek protected and maintained for public use. But he was also serious about the company's need for cash to build new ski lifts. We had the land appraised for $600,000, a startling number at the time, and Janss eventually agreed to a one-year $10,000 exclusive option to purchase on a bargain sale price of $470,000: $50,000 down, $100,000 in one year, and the balance in two. We had a deal.

In the meantime, however, Jack and I had walked the Fish and Game lands that his commission managed downstream and were generally appalled at the trash, the overgrazing of the stream banks, and enthusiasm for "put and take" hatchery practices that were gradually industrializing one of the rare great spring creeks in the west. He admitted that public ownership would make a long-term program of research, restoration, and conservation difficult. It seemed a waste to turn it over to the state. In a moment of weakness, I agreed to launch a $600,000 fundraising program to complete the initial research and acquisition and maintain the property in private Conservancy ownership. But on one condition: Jack Hemingway, with his vast network of the rich and famous, would chair the fundraising committee. "I hate asking people for money," Jack said, "but let's do it!"

Some of my Conservancy colleagues were aghast at the idea of kowtowing to stars, the Sun Valley crowd, and hobbyist fly-fishermen. They marshaled their arguments. For starters, we had never raised more than $10,000 in Idaho, a backwater of environmental philanthropy if ever there was one, much less $600,000. "And rainbow trout are hardly endangered!" said Bob Jenkins, The Nature Conservancy vice-president for science. Jenkins was a PhD from Harvard who determined what was ecologically important based on mountains of data and mapped "element occurrences," small tracts around the country where university botanists and agency herpetologists knew there were endangered plants, rare reptiles, and such. The idea was to use the scarce funds to purchase such priority sites. It was an important strategy that set The Nature Conservancy apart from other land conservation groups—conservation based on science and not just sentiment.

But the only "occurrences" on Silver Creek were Ernest Hemingway, Gary Cooper, Jane Mansfield and the other celebrities that fly-fished and duck-hunted there. "Great," I countered. "So much the better for raising the money necessary to fuel its acquisition and launching more substantial conservation efforts down the road." I probably had them with "money," but couldn't help adding, "And, by the way, caddis and mayflies know good habitat when they see it."

So launch we did. My boss in San Francisco, Henry Little, told me, however, that I was in way over my ahead and would need his help. In reality, he was also a fly-fisherman and wanted to be able to be part of saving Silver Creek and fish in the course of work. I could hardly blame him. He suggested we go to George Gund, a part-time Sun Valley resident with an old pile of money from Cleveland's Kaffee Hag Corporation, makers of decaffeinated coffee. George was a strapping hockey player, a big handsome guy, but was notoriously soft-spoken—so much so that when Henry met with George over lunch in Sun Valley, he wasn't sure, after delivering his pitch and hearing George's reply, whether or not a pledge had been clearly made. Henry had been too reluctant to press him on it.

So we scheduled another lunch meeting. The plan was to tell George about our desperate need for $50,000 toward meeting the down-payment deadline. We strategically sat on either side of him so that, when we asked him for the pledge, we could

Farming near Silver Creek. The fine-loess, wind-blown soil filled in the creek when pushed to the edges of the stream.

actually hear the answer. Henry made the pitch: "George, we need $50,000 to make this go. What do you think?" George muttered something or other, and Henry and I said, almost in unison, "$50,000! That would be great!" We were pretty sure he'd said it and, sure enough, he was good for it. Soft-spoken, generous George saved Silver Creek, right then and there.

There was more, of course. Jack Hemingway had agreed to round up a blue-ribbon fundraising committee, people he knew from his Paris and New York Anglers Club days—people like Charles Ritz, as in the hotel. Weeks later I called Jack to see how he was doing. "Did Charles Ritz join the committee?"

"Yes, he's on, everyone's on."

Everyone? My antennae went up. "When did you talk with him?"

"Well, I didn't exactly, but I'll tell him next time I'm in Paris."

And thus we assembled a very distinguished, world-class fundraising committee for Silver Creek. The Conservancy brass were duly impressed.

And so it went. John Fery, an affable and leading businessman known to enjoy fishing Silver Creek, was Chairman of Boise Cascade, one of the largest forest products companies in the country that was known neither for its enthusiasm for environmental causes nor the magnitude of its corporate philanthropy. But Boise's head of corporate giving was a distant cousin of mine, Mary Malarkey. With Mary's help and John's enthusiasm for Silver Creek, we eventually teed up a $100,000 cash gift to meet another down-payment—this in exchange for the enthusiastic public profile Boise Cascade rightly deserved: it was their largest gift ever and their first for conservation. Fery wanted press, so we discussed people I might be able to "deliver" for the press conference, scheduled for live TV on the banks of Silver Creek. I suggested Robert Redford or Idaho governor Cecil Andrus, but Fery considered Redford too "radical" and Andrus too close, so we opted for Oregon's Governor Tom McCall, who had just joined the Conservancy's national board of governors.

Governor McCall and I flew to Boise, where Fery had Boise Cascade's corporate jet ready for the hop to Hailey. But Governor McCall got sidelined with a television reporter on some issue of the day. Fery, who by this time was probably wishing we'd gone for the less loquacious Redford, grew impatient and finally said that if we weren't on the plane in five minutes he'd cancel the press conference. I had no rank to pull, so I gently pulled on McCall instead: "Let's go, Governor. We're about to miss the plane!"

So we show up on the hillside above the stream with a TV crew in tow and respective speeches in hand to talk about Boise's extraordinary gift and how the Conservancy was going to restore the stream from years of overgrazing cows. The cameras are rolling, panning out over the countryside—just in time to catch several hundred cows grazing leisurely over the whole preserve! Someone had cut a fence for the greener grass on the other side and to test the new owner's management. I hastily directed the cameras to a prairie falcon in a long swoop over the opposite horizon and tried to wax eloquent about the compatibility of conservation and farming. The Conservancy brass had a fit about the cows, but Boise Cascade and John Fery had their day in the sun and their support helped meet yet another critical deadline.

Research confirmed that Silver Creek was indeed in steep ecological decline: years of intensive farming and grazing too close to the banks had blown the fine-loess soils into the stream, gradually covering the gravel spawning beds, with cattle eating small willows and streamside vegetation, thus widening and warming the streams, reducing the depth and richness of its native moss beds, and threatening the health of the entire aquatic ecosystem. But when the streams were fenced and farm fields backed off the stream banks, it was extraordinary how quickly Silver Creek and its "music" were revived.

And as things turned out, my extemporaneous spiel about conservation and farming wasn't entirely groundless. In 1977, I hired Guy Bonnivier as the Silver Creek Preserve manager. Guy did a terrific job connecting with the neighbors and, over the ensuing years, successfully worked with

27

important ranchers and farmers like Bud Purdy and gradually extended acquisitions and conservation easements to protect over 10,000 acres of the Silver Creek headwaters. We built a strong base of support in the Sun Valley community, put our offices in the old Hemingway home in Ketchum, which Mary Hemingway kindly left to the Conservancy in her will, and became a strong voice for rational conservation and agricultural development throughout the state.

Both the Sandy River and the Silver Creek projects provided me a chance to get my feet wet—literally—in the service of the kind of traditional land preservation that was and is The Nature Conservancy's honorable hallmark: save the "best of the rest" and the "last of the least." It sounded good to me and was enormously satisfying. At this stage, in fact, I couldn't imagine an alternative approach in the face of what I still perceived as the enemy—encroaching development. I was green in more

Bud Purdy, 90, farmer and donor of thousands of acres of conservation easement lands that helped protect Silver Creek.

ways than one, but I'd at least learned about how and how not to approach perspective donors and recruit them to the cause. That the "cause" itself might be insufficient to the real task at hand was something I'd learn only later—the hard way.

Degraded streambank of a Silver Creek tributary.

Restoration underway with private landowners, by former Silver Creek Preserve manager, Guy Bonnivier.

29

2

TWO RANCHES: *Cowboys and Conservationists*

As I sat in Room 26 of the Tabard Inn that cold January day mulling over our letter of resignation to The Nature Conservancy, it was both clear and important to me that our decision was not the result of a mere personality clash. Over my years both in the Northwest and then the International Program, I'd developed great respect for the growing number of colleagues at the Conservancy, even those like Vice President for Science Bob Jenkins—he of the "element occurrences"—with whom I often disagreed. If there were differences about the strategic relationship between the national headquarters and the growing International Program, I had been sure that Pete Seligmann and I could iron them out, and we'd had countless meetings at the Conservancy's headquarters in Arlington trying to do just that.

Still, it was clear to me—at least in hindsight—that a more perceptive or objective observer might well have seen this coming, even years earlier. Certainly, this was not the first time I'd locked horns with the folks at the national office. Two previous occasions that stand out both involved ranches— one a dude ranch and the other an operating cattle ranch. In both cases, it came down to a clash between sticking with the predetermined game plan versus adapting to the situation on the ground. Nature, of course, is famous for adapting; bureaucrats not so much. And The Nature Conservancy's game plan had not foreseen accommodating either dudes or cowboys.

Pine Butte Swamp, Montana

The inspiration for the Pine Butte Swamp preserve, as well as for its outdoor education program and wilderness research, sprang largely from the aura and persona of John J. Craighead. Craighead is a famous grizzly biologist who, as I write this, is 93 and living at home with his wife, Margaret, in Missoula. John and his twin brother Frank had been heroes of mine since grade school, when I followed their writings and took up the art and practice of falconry. Their families are some of the great wilderness researchers, authors, filmmakers, photographers, hunters and fishermen, and outdoorsmen in America. John and Frank devoted their lives to pioneering research with birds of prey and large carnivores in mountain wilderness ecosystems in western North America, and the only place in the lower 48 where grizzlies were known to reinhabit the prairie was Pine Butte Swamp, a large fen, or slow-flowing bog, on the Rocky Mountain Front.

Ranching on the Rocky Mountain Front.

In 1977, the U.S. Fish & Wildlife Service and the State of Montana identified Pine Butte Swamp as a "unique ecosystem" of national importance and therefore worthy of protection. The swamp was a network of grasslands and beaver ponds ringed with willows and wild rose, perfect habitat for dozens of bird species, and perhaps most important, the grizzly bear that summered there. It represented some of the last lowland range of an animal that actually evolved on the great plains, as well as in the alpine environment where our long siege on wilderness has pushed them.

In the meantime, however, test sites were being developed for oil drilling in Pine Butte Swamp, which is part of the over-thrust belt—a geologic system of faults in which rock layers have been pushed over one another by tectonic forces within the earth's crust—and possibly rich in oil and gas. Nothing, of course, could be more antithetical to preserving the summering habitat of rare plains grizzly bear and dancing grounds for sharp-tail grouse—or, in the opinion of many ranchers, the traditional lifestyle of the range—than a network of roads, rigs, cables, and ponds filled with drilling mud. The stakes were clear, and The Nature Conservancy went into action like the light cavalry that we were in those days.

The 30,000-acre Salmond family ranch was a key part of the corridor of lands necessary to connect the vast Bob Marshall Wilderness Area with Pine Butte Swamp. Ken Margolis, who had been doing important conservation work in Montana for years, dispatched me to take a look and see if we might acquire it for something less than the $25 million asking price—a stretch for us, though we might find a way to make it work. And as an added bonus, I might have an opportunity to finally meet John Craighead. Needless to say, I jumped at the chance.

In my enthusiasm, I jumped a bit too quickly, arriving at the Portland airport just in time for the flight but realizing at the last minute that I'd neglected to bring my wallet. Not a propitious start, but with a ticket to Great Falls gripped tightly in my hand and Napoleon's "Commit, then figure it out!" ringing in my head, I was off to Montana.

At the Great Falls airport, a Hertz representative was unmoved by my Napoleonic fervor and seemed dubious, even, about my qualifications as a member of the species: "No wallet? No license? No credit card?" she intoned incredulously. "Sorry, sir."

But "sorry" wasn't going to cut it. Alice Salmond, matriarch of a family of cowboys, would be waiting for me at the Log Cabin Drive-In Restaurant in the small western town of Choteau at noon. I'd have to hitchhike.

Big Sky. Empty roads. The only driver too lonely to pass me up was leaning over the wheel of an old black Cadillac hearse. The ride was fine, but I did ask him to let me out a block short of the Log Cabin, lest Mrs. Salmond think I couldn't be trusted to come up with $25 million—not that we felt it was worth anything close to that. The negotiations would be key.

She was waiting for me at the restaurant, a wonderful white-haired woman in her seventies, rosy cheeked and sympathetic to, if a bit skeptical of, her prospective buyer. It was raining hard with a warm Chinook wind on top of spring snowmelt as we drove 20 miles on muddy ranch roads through rolling grasslands, cattle grazing in willow bottoms, and the high, rugged Rocky Mountain Front rising steadily on the western horizon. Mrs. Salmond dropped me off at her son Jim's ranch house, where I bunked with the family. We had dinner and stale coffee and cowboy talk, but the chance to negotiate never arose that night. Jim said, "Just come down for breakfast and I'll show you around the place."

Breakfast the next morning came to the linoleum kitchen table long before the sun came up on the eastern horizon. There were piles of eggs and bacon and toast. Hardly a word was spoken. Jim nodded to one teenage son to load up some horses and get them to the Deep Creek corrals. The younger son received similar Morse code for firing up a D-7 bulldozer and cleaning up another back road toward the same mysterious high mountain location. Without wanting to break into talk and ask, I deduced that a roundup was in the works on the Salmond Ranch.

Jim drove me in the pickup to show me around to some of the sights hard by the Rocky Mountain Front, weaving the same long north-south trail as millennia of Beringians used in migrating from Asia across the Bering Sea Land Bridge to populate the Americas. Eventually we found ourselves coming around a high mountain bend in the road in driving, freezing rain and foot-deep ruts on a one-lane road of slick clay whose shoulder fell steeply downhill into Deep Creek. We got there just in time to see several cowboys on horseback pushing a dozen reluctant cattle into a jury-rigged corral on the creek bottom, only to have a bull drive a large hole in one side of the corral and head over the hill with the hard-won cows in hot pursuit, followed by several mad cowboys whooping invectives at the Almighty and anyone else within earshot. They all disappeared across rolling prairie in fog and rain. I was agog, but Jim took it all in stride: just another day on the ranch.

In the meantime, a pickup with a large black bull in the back had arrived and was sliding down the greasy mountain road in front of us, dangerously close to tipping over the bank, teetering from one side to the other as the bull charged about trying to bolt the whole arrangement and follow his brethren over the horizon. One angry, dirty, over-sized cowboy jumped out from behind the wheel with a three-foot section of pipe. He climbed up on the hood of the truck and began bludgeoning the bloody bull into better behavior. We hooked a chain to the front of his pickup and backed up, all four wheels spitting mud to try to pull him out, only to have our own rear-end almost swing over the bank as well.

Next, a cowboy on a tractor was called into action from a nearby barn and he got the bull and pickup all rolling down the road nicely, only to have the tractor skid over the bank with the whole show, headed steeply downhill straight toward a deteriorating barn. Old man and patriarch JC Salmond, strong as an ox in his 70s, had by this time appeared on the scene and shouted for someone to open a gate just in time for the whole train of tractor, pickup, and mad bloody bull to slide gracefully through to the creek bottom.

That mission accomplished, we headed back to the home place with the big bull and a few cows finally loaded up in a large cattle truck on a road much improved by the 14-year-old on the D-7, and I tried to casually bring up my own mission to Jim.

Jim just as casually lauded the landscape and mentioned something about selling just part of the ranch for $25 million, cash. We were rounding a bend as I took this in and happened to look back just in time to see the cattle truck sliding over a small bridge, down a bank, and tipping over into a willow bottom, spewing bruised and confused cattle across the creek bed. I ran back to the overturned truck, now spilling gas out of the tank, and pulled a worried sheepdog, spare chains, and a fire extinguisher off the top of the now-bloody and unconscious driver lying in a heap on top of the right window. He woke up with a string of curses just as JC came around the bend in full swing on the back of his horse. I helped the cowboy out, and he wiped blood off his face with a tattered coat sleeve while running for a saddle horse that another teenage cowboy had loosed from a truck nearby. They all headed off through the brush—horses, JC, cowboys of all ages—with the weary cattle once again headed over the prairie horizon, while the 14-year-old backed the D-7 up to salvage the overturned truck. I was beginning to feel the way I had on my first visit to New York City: surely these people are doing this to impress tourists; they can't possibly keep this up all year round!

We got back to the ranch house in time for lunch, where, around the same linoleum kitchen table, silent but muddy family members all acted as if it had been a perfectly normal morning, never betraying the slightest acknowledgment that the whole show was for sale to the wide-eyed, wallet-less conservationist from Portland.

We never did put together a deal on the Salmond's ranch, though David Letterman later did. He now owns a gorgeous part of it, works with the Conservancy on the Rocky Mountain Front, and jets in from New York for long weekends of solitude with friends and family. He and the Salmond family have worked together with the ranching and conservation community to protect the rich character of ancient Beringians, cows, and wildlife of Big Sky Country.

Looking west at Pine Butte and the Rocky Mountains.

What we did accomplish, however, was the assembly of almost 20,000 acres from a half-dozen individual ranches of adjacent acres of rolling grasslands, wetlands, a high butte, dinosaur digs, and buffalo jumps now called the Pine Butte Swamp Preserve of The Nature Conservancy. Over the course of several years—negotiating the purchase of these various tracts of land, raising the money, and beginning to develop a management plan—I stayed at the nearby Circle 8 Guest Ranch. Kenny and Alice Gleason had homesteaded 2,800 acres on the South Fork of the Teton River between the swamp and the wilderness in the 1920s and '30s. When I asked Kenny why he homesteaded the Circle 8 Ranch for guests instead of cattle, he replied, "Dudes are easier to winter." They had built up a loyal group of several hundred guests who came and rode Tennessee Walker horses, fished, and relaxed in eight separate cabins and a big log dining lodge, all of which Kenny had built by hand. They took hunting and scenic pack trips into Gates Park in the Bob Marshall Wilderness when the aspen are golden in the fall. I had plenty of time visiting with Kenny and Alice, often being their only guest in the off-season, and they became co-conspirators in putting together the preserve. As we talked, it became apparent that Kenny and Alice wanted to see the Circle 8 preserved as well. The Nature Conservancy, on its current Web site, proclaims that it "takes great pride in carrying on the Gleason's Circle 8 tradition of hospitality, comfort and friendliness as well as respect for the magnificent country that surrounds the ranch."

I have no doubt this pride is genuine, but in 1978, the Conservancy brass in Washington were more than a little skeptical about owning a dude ranch, complete with cabins, horses, and regular guests. I made the case that gathering crucial information about moose, elk, and grizzly was as essential as undisturbed habitat on the Front Range. The Circle 8, I further argued, would be ideal for Conservancy donors and members and an excellent base camp for research in the entire Northern Rockies wilderness ecosystem. The brass bought it and we bought the Circle 8, subject to a life estate for the Gleasons.

And yes, I did finally get to meet my boyhood idol, John Craighead. John has a big winning smile, a bear hug, and an inextinguishable twinkle in his eye. The photo of him at 90 that

The Nature Conservancy's Circle 8 Guest Ranch near Choteau, Montana.

37

Peter Burrell, the author, John Craighead, and Constance Mellon on top of Pine Butte.

accompanies this story pretty much says it all, so I'll just add that, over the many years I've known him, John has always seemed to me as much an alpha grizzly as the many he studied in Yellowstone National Park. Also, needless to say, it was a privilege for me to work with him on the Pine Butte Swamp project.

Our big fundraising opportunity involving John came when the late Mrs. Richard King "Constance" Mellon expressed an interest in preserving grizzlies, meeting John, and seeing Pine Butte Swamp—not necessarily in that order. A clutch of her advisors—along with Conservancy President Pat Noonan and her second husband, Peter Burrell, who was English and was said to have been the "Queen's Horseman"—all climbed aboard the family plane in Pittsburgh and flew to Great Falls. We'd timed it carefully at the peak of the fall color and they arrived on a crisp cobalt blue sky evening with fresh snow in the high peaks. John, of course, was the expert of honor and we planned a long ride in the morning to the top of Pine Butte, fully aware that both Mr. Burrell and Mrs. Mellon loved horses. That night we packed an impressive picnic lunch. We were locked and loaded.

The next morning we awoke to fresh snow, grey skies, and frigid temperatures. Mrs. Mellon took one look out the window and said, "You don't need to saddle my horse!" John and I were devastated; we needed the support of the Mellon Foundation to complete critical acquisitions. So we saddled up a couple of pick up trucks instead and convinced the matron to come for a short drive. Crossing a wet meadow at the foot of the Butte, we almost immediately buried the truck up to its hubs in mud, wheels whirring without effect. Mrs. Mellon was not impressed. Despite her wanting to turn right back to the guest ranch, we got another pickup and eventually found our way to the top of the Butte.

As we sat on a high rock, John described the qualities of this unique wetland prairie habitat as only someone with his knowledge and background could. It was as masterful and nearly as moving as the vista itself, and this time Mrs. Mellon *was* impressed. She turned to me and, with a hand sweeping across the enormous expanse, asked, "How much for all this?"

"Four million," I said, and shut up.

"I'll give you $3 million."

Well done, John!

The Nature Conservancy has successfully operated the Circle 8 and the Pine Butte Swamp Preserve for 30 years. In the summer of 2007, Montana State Director Jamie Williams gathered key donors together at the Circle 8 to discuss land conservation priorities for the Rocky Mountain Front. By the end of the weekend he'd raised over $25 million in new commitments, including an extraordinary $15 million gift from The Richard King Mellon Foundation, to pursue conservation along the entire 350,000-acre front range.

Ranchers and dudes can be good for conservation.

John J. Craighead, age 91, at home in Missoula.

39

Sycan Marsh, Oregon

March 1977, The Nature Conservancy Northwest Office, Portland, Oregon: the office manager caught my eye as I entered.

"Spencer, there's someone on the phone. Says his name is Hawk Hyde."

"I'll take that one," I said, and headed for my desk.

Hawk Hyde. Just the name took me back 10 years to when my friend Donny Kerr and I wanted to photograph nesting goshawks during our spring break from college.

Goshawks are a relatively rare and reclusive species regarded as the hawk of all hawks—but we had few ideas where to find them. If anyone would know, I figured it would be Tom McAllister, who would eventually become our trusty guide and fundraiser for the Sandy River project.

"The Yamsi Ranch, of course," Tom said without hesitation, east of Klamath Falls, near Sycan Marsh. The Yamsi's owner was Dayton Hyde, he said, known as "Hawk." "Stanford educated, writer, and cowboy. But he dislikes interlopers, so I better write you a letter of introduction."

So Donny and I headed south with the letter and camping and photography gear packed into the back of Dad's old red Land Rover. Also along were Zeno and Zaleski, two fledgling great horned owls we'd pulled from a nest in a tall poplar tree along the upper John Day earlier that year.

"Watch the birdie." Zeno, a young great horned owl, on the author's head while camped on the banks of the Williamson River, Yamsi Ranch.

It was hot and dusty when we arrived at the Yamsi Ranch headquarters, nestled into picturesque lodge pole pine at the headwaters of the trout-filled Williamson River. Hawk's wife, Gerta, directed us to nearby corrals where there was some sort of roundup under way. We walked sheepishly to a log-rail fence holding ornery cattle and like-tempered cowboys on horseback. We might as well have been invisible—two lost tourist kids unworthy of so much as a glance. Ten minutes passed, 20, 30. We were beginning to feel a little rejected, but our goshawk adventure depended upon Hawk Hyde, so we waited.

Finally, Hawk—a well-sculpted, tall, tanned man in Levi's and boots—approached and eyed us as if we were prey of some sort.

"What do you guys want?"

"We're friends of Tom McAllister. He wrote you this note." Hawk looked at it briefly then fixed us firmly in his steely gaze.

"Who the hell is Tom McAllister?"

Dead silence. And then he laughed.

Recovered, we told him about the young owls in the back of our Land Rover and our hopes of photographing goshawks. Hawk shared our interest, pointed us in the right direction, and showed us a gorgeous campsite on the ranch. We tented and fished in a meadow along the meandering Williamson River for four or five days with Zeno and Zaleski flying freely about camp. We also found and photographed the goshawks.

That was the beginning of a long friendship with Dayton O.

Adult female goshawk feeding her chicks, the Hyde's Yamsi Ranch, 1967.

Hyde, though I could not for the life of me imagine why he would be calling The Nature Conservancy office 10 years later. I found out as soon as I got to my desk and picked up the phone:

"Hawk! How are you?"

"Sycan Marsh is for sale. You're gonna help me save it." Hawk isn't big on small talk.

Sycan Marsh: a 33,000-acre, 5,000-foot-elevation Serengeti of a marsh, with hundreds of nesting going sandhill cranes, goshawks, great grey owls, and old-growth sugar pine. And cows. And dikes, ditches, and fences. It was the summer pasture for the ZX Ranch, the largest in the Northwest. Oh, and Weyerhaeuser's logging railroad running right down the middle. Seemed doable.

"What's the asking price?"

"Eight million cash, subject to continued grazing."

"And the owner?"

The "level grassy place" that is Sycan Marsh.

"Nicolas Salgo, a tough Hungarian business man. Lives in a fancy apartment next to Central Park in New York. Owns the Watergate in Washington, D.C., too."

"Uh-huh. Hawk, this is gonna be tougher than photographing

angry goshawks at the nest." Buy an operating ranch? That has to stay in operation? "No sane person at the Conservancy is gonna go for this."

"Yeah. That's why I called you instead." Cowboy humor.

I still had one foot in the Silver Creek project, but this was too outlandish a prospect to pass up. A little research and a few phone calls later, I was off to the Watergate to have lunch with Mr. Salgo at his French restaurant, Jean Louis—slightly more upscale than my usual lunch counter in northwest Portland. I walked in wearing jeans to meet this millionaire in a chalk-stripe blue suit. Nicolas Salgo, an eastern European Jew who fled Hitler, had had a dream of owning a piece of the American West. And before he died in 2005 at the age of 90, he owned more than a piece—over 1.3 million acres of grassland, desert, and high meadow, forest, and marshland in southern Oregon—the largest ranch in the Northwest.

He'd built a huge multicompany conglomerate called Bangor Punta that owned diverse companies like Smith and Wesson, Starcraft boats, and Piper, the aircraft manufacturer. Later, President Reagan appointed him ambassador to Hungary.

Much of the time I had no idea what he was talking about with his strong Hungarian accent and his rapid rundowns of complex financing. But I liked him; he was decisive and uncompromising.

I managed to get an exclusive one-year option to purchase Sycan Marsh for $5 million subject to a 40-year leaseback for grazing at fair market value. That would be almost $150,000 in annual grazing lease income. I figured the Conservancy could build a stewardship endowment with it, then develop a serious program of research, drive hard on grazing practices, and demonstrate that conservation and ranching might go together after all.

Henry Little, my boss in the Western Regional Office, and headquarters staff wanted nothing to do with it. The water rights alone were very complex and took a platoon of lawyers to work out. Bob Jenkins, as usual, was the most vocal. "Even if we wanted Sycan, which we don't, where would we come up with $5 million?"

"How about the Goodhill Foundation?" I suggested.

Talk about tossing fuel on a fire. Jenkins had just come upon a treasure trove at the Goodhill Foundation: $42 million left in the will of an extraordinary charitable 3M heiress named Catherine Ordway, who had shown up in Washington, D.C., in the early 1970s. Nature Conservancy lore has it that Ms. Ordway, a shy, plainly dressed older woman, had arrived unannounced at various conservation organization headquarters asking to see the president. Rebuffed by several, she showed up at the Conservancy's National Office to see Pat Noonan, our own affable and infinitely clever president, who said, "Send her up." Then he sent a quick note to his development department asking them who Catherine Ordway was. The note came back with a succinct directive: "3M Pay Attention."

"What can I do for you, Miss Ordway?" said Pat.

"I'm from the Midwest," she said, "and I'm worried about the loss of native prairies. I'd like to help save them."

"I see," he said. "What did you have in mind?"

"I want to save a prairie as far as the eye can see," said Ms. Ordway. "At my diminutive height I figure that would be about 10,000 acres—perhaps a million dollars."

The Nature Conservancy had never heard of a million dollars at that time in our early history. Noonan, trying not to fall off his chair, said he thought a million would be fine.

"We'll be right back to you with a million-dollar prairie," he said as he showed her graciously to the door, behind which he almost danced in glee.

It took a long time to find a native prairie in the entire Midwest; most were along fenced-in railroad right-of-ways and pioneer cemeteries, which was all that seemed to be left behind by the vast herds of cattle that followed on the heels of the vanishing bison herds. But eventually, Noonan and Jenkins found large tracts of prairie, and the gentle Miss Ordway donated over $40 million for a national system, the Ordway Prairie Preserves, before she died in a small house with a leaky roof in Connecticut in 1975.

Perhaps appropriately, Jenkins thought he owned the Goodhill Foundation, which was directed to spend itself out of existence to benefit land conservation across the country. And it helped that one of the three Goodhill Foundation trustees was a renowned older gentleman named Richard Pough, who had long ties to the Conservancy. Unbeknownst to me, Dick had visited Sycan with Hawk Hyde on a beautiful spring day in 1979, right about the time I was trying to imagine where we might find a crisp 5-million dollar bill. Hawk drove Dick to the top of a high volcanic butte southwest of Sycan at sunset, where they watched a golden eagle swoop by so close that the wind whistled through its primaries—the flight feathers along the edge of the bird's wing. Dancing sandhill cranes rolling their romantic call, ducks and geese by the thousands, a distant cowboy pushing a few mooing cows ahead of a heavy trail of dust. Dick Pough was enchanted.

Meanwhile, scientific pride and politics were holding sway over my efforts to get the board to approve acquisition of Sycan Marsh. It didn't help that I'd already accepted an offer to move with my family to Washington to develop the Conservancy's International Program, weakening my pull in the Western Regional Office. Right now, time was running out and Salgo threatened to pull out if the deal wasn't concluded soon. He was trying to sell the entire ZX Ranch to an insurance company that had little interest in complicated land titles and interfering environmentalists who wanted the swamp in the middle of the ranch.

The Conservancy board's land acquisition committee had its quarterly meeting. More of a showdown, actually. The acquisition committee meetings were the heart of The Nature Conservancy's operations, where the up or down vote on whether or not to buy a piece of land was made. Typically, you had to have the whole package lined up: it had to be ecologically significant; you had to have the hard deal; and you had to know where the money was coming from. I had only two of the three unequivocally, at least at the time, but in my corner I had a few critical Conservancy brass, including President Pat Noonan and Dave Morine, vice-president for land acquisition. In truth, Noonan and Morine knew little about nature, but they loved the art of the deal and this was a big one—one of the largest in the Conservancy's history till then.

Unfortunately, Pat, like myself, had also announced his resignation and was therefore something of a lame duck.

I passed around aerial photos taken out of Danny Vollum's helicopter. Jenkins scowled; "Looks like an overgrazed pasture to me."

Jenkins was right; it was a pasture. But it was also the only 30,000-acre high-altitude marsh in the lower 48 left with any semblance of intact ecosystem. As far as the grazing rights, I said, "It's going to cash flow $150,000 a year. Just collect the rent and put it in the bank. Then you've got a stewardship endowment. Use the income from the endowment to do research and improve grazing practices and conservation outcomes. The project is self-funding."

Robert Anderson—board member, New Mexico rancher, and son of Arco's Chairman Robert O. Anderson—took the bait. Bob loved the idea of the Conservancy learning to work with ranchers and rural economies. He made a great speech about this being "the very symbol of a new breed of conservation" and about how, in 40 years, our grandchildren would thank us. Dave Morine and Pat Noonan nodded approvingly, but Jenkins' face was growing as red as his hair. My suggestion that Goodhill funds would pay for the deal held no sway for the hard science that drove Conservancy decision-making and his own list of priority projects. The showdown at the Yamsi corral was starting to get ugly

Yellow rail, banded at Sycan Marsh in 2005 during a research study.

when, to everyone's surprise, including my own, in walks Goodhill trustee Dick Pough.

"Sycan Marsh? My God, I've seen it with my own eyes. There's nothing like it in the entire country. The Goodhill Foundation will put up 100 percent of the funds!"

And so with Pat, Dave, and Robert Anderson's help it was approved: $5 million cash for 26,000 acres, most of Sycan Marsh, subject to a

40-year lease back to the ZX to carry on the ranching pride of the American west. After Sycan was "saved," rare upland sandpipers and endangered nesting populations of the diminutive yellow rail were discovered there, just one of a handful of such populations in the entire West; even Bob Jenkins would have to call that an "occurrence." A research station was later built with the generous support of the M. J. Murdock

Dick Mecham, ZX Ranch manager in 2008, Paisley, Oregon.

Charitable Trust, most of the remainder of Sycan was acquired, and bird-watching Conservancy donors from far and wide became periodic visitors. When we bought Sycan in 1980, there were five species of nesting ducks. Now there are 14. Freshwater mussels are recovering along with red band trout and threatened bull trout. Miller Lake lamprey were thought to be extinct but are now increasingly common at Sycan. The Forest Service, Klamath Indian Tribe, and State Forestry Department are working with the Conservancy on prescribed burning programs to reduce the risk of catastrophic fire and improve forest ecosystem health and species diversity.

In 2004, the Conservancy renegotiated the lease with the ZX Ranch, then owned by 94-year-old potato king J. R. Simplot and managed by an affable man named Dick Mecham. Just 8,000 of the Conservancy's almost 30,000 acres are grazed, leaving the rest to wetland and native grassland restoration. Dikes and ditches are being filled in and head gates removed. Sensitive streams are being fenced and the recovery of riparian willow, aspen, and cottonwood in just a few years is remarkable.

And the folks at the ZX ranch seem to be happy. Additional fencing has made it easier to manage herding behavior, allowing the cows to be moved more frequently with less attention from the cowboys. The quality of the grass is higher, meaning the same number of cows can graze on a smaller area. Current Sycan manager Craig Beinz says that calf weight gain has increased sub-stantially, while pregnancy rates of mother cows has increased from 48 percent to 97 percent, for an estimated net gain to the ZX of some $500,000 annually in increased value of the herd. Nesting sandhill cranes roll their distinctive calls, while cowboys and con-servationists are pushing a few purebreds together down a less dusty trail. In the evening, a high volcanic cinder cone casts shad-ows over a vast wetland like nowhere else on Earth.

For me, the Sycan project was an early inkling that ecology and economy might not be the natural enemies I'd assumed they were, that maybe conservationists and developers actually could work side by side to get what they both wanted. Was I beginning to believe the rhetoric I'd spontaneously spouted for the camera-men at Silver Creek or the speech that Bob Anderson had made to the acquisitions committee? Not quite, but a seed had been planted that would grow—not in Oregon or Idaho or Montana, but on foreign soil to the south.

Before and after photographs of the Conservancy's stream restoration work at Sycan Marsh. Fencing to exclude cattle grazing shows a dramatic and sudden result in improved riparian vegetation and aquatic habitat.

3

SOUTH OF THE BORDER: *Releasing Local Energy*

Back at the Tabard Inn, it occurred to me—it could hardly have not occurred to me—that had it not been for The Nature Conservancy's interest in an International Program, I might at this very moment have been meeting new people and finding new land to save in the six Northwestern states rather than resigning to start a totally new and competing organization called Conservation International. Certainly, when The Nature Conservancy president Pat Noonan had, late in 1979, asked me to move to Washington, D.C., to develop the new international program, I'd had definite misgivings about it. Janie and I were settled into a new home in Portland with three young children, and uprooting the family for such a major change was not an appealing prospect. But a new frontier with important opportunities was somehow impossible to turn down.

And so in August of 1980, we piled into the old VW bus and headed east. We stopped in Telluride, Colorado, to visit an old college friend of Janie's, then continued east. The cool mountain air of the Colorado Plateau gradually warmed as we descended from the Rockies, it grew hotter as we progressed across late summer rangeland of the eastern plain, and the humidity rose continuously across the Midwest. By the time we reached our new home in Leesburg, Virginia, 30 miles west of the nation's capital, it was hot—90 degrees and 90 percent humidity in the sultry, languorous summer, south of the Mason Dixon Line. That there might be some symbolism in this was not a notion I entertained.

The New Assignment

As the director of The Nature Conservancy's International Program, my assignment was to figure out what, if anything, to do in the New World tropics—the "neotropics"—of Latin America. It was a daunting task. God knows I was as keen as anyone else about saving wild land, but there was no wild land in Latin America and hadn't been for many thousands of years. Indigenous people lived on and by the land virtually everywhere. Firewood for cooking and building came from nearby forests; streams provided drinking water; food was grown on small plots scattered about the forest. Waves of colonial farmers practicing subsistence livelihoods on the edge of survival meant that millions of rural people depended upon the well-being of the environment. While the ecosystems might not be pristine, they were still incredibly rich in biodiversity—there were more species of birds in many single national parks in these countries than in all of North America. Despite the challenges, we could hardly stand by and do nothing.

During the first few months I searched for people and expertise in Washington to guide me, but could find little encouragement. Among the big international agencies—World Bank, U.S. Agency for International Development (USAID), and prominent international nongovernmental organizations like World Wildlife Fund (WWF)—I found it difficult to identify a coherent strategy about what international organizations might do to effectively promote long-term conservation and development in the neotropics. Peter Raven, charismatic scientist and director of the Missouri Botanical Garden, made a compelling case for the importance of the tropics for biodiversity and the challenges presented by growing global populations and deep poverty in developing countries. Tom Lovejoy at WWF was doing critical scientific research in Amazonian Brazil showing that bigger is better for protected areas in tropical rain forest ecosystems. But with a staff of 40, WWF had few Latin American professionals in-house and, indeed, few staff who spoke Spanish. About the development agencies, one of the more provocative thoughts I found was in a book called *We Don't Know How,* by William Paddock, which essentially said that the big American success stories for agricultural and community development around the world were empty propaganda, blown life-size for the benefit of congressional appropriations. It looked like fresh territory.

There was, however, a very bright light. I found Jack Hood Vaughn, former director of the Peace Corps, later U.S. ambassador in Colombia and Panama, under-secretary of state for Latin America, and in his youth, a lightweight professional prizefighter. As a marine in the Pacific theater in World War II, Jack had survived three bullet wounds in the buttocks—all clear evidence of the direction he was running at the time, he told me. But he was a war hero nevertheless.

And my hero as well. When I first met Jack, he was serving as acting director of USAID—"acting," Jack explained, because Senator Jesse Helms told the Senate Foreign Relations Committee that "Jack Vaughn is a communist, abortionist, and worst of all, an environmentalist." He was never confirmed as director of USAID, which was fine with him. I'd met Jack before, but only briefly—at Peace Corps training in Camp Crozier, Puerto Rico, a dozen years earlier in 1968. It was at training—hot, humid, and sticky. Puerto Rico felt loud, noisy, chaotic, and buggy. I was learning Spanish for the first time. The whole Peace Corps thing sounded interesting, but, for the first time in my life, I was disoriented and my morale wasn't high. I was thinking, "I've gotta change my whole life here and start thinking about people instead of birds."

And then Jack came through the camp one afternoon and did this pep talk—told us what this was all about. I'd never heard anybody speak like Jack. He was tough, he was smart, he was funny; he made it sound like we could save the world. He had the whole camp on fire.

51

Jack became my inside source for all things both humorous and thought provoking in Washington. He knew not only the existing and former Latin American presidents, their wives, friends, and enemies, but also their girlfriends. As former director of the Peace Corps after its founding by President Kennedy and early leadership by Kennedy's brother-in-law

Ambassador Jack Hood Vaughn.

Sergeant Shriver, Jack also knew something about volunteers and soon became a board member of The Nature Conservancy and chair of the volunteer committee. It was great to have him on board, and I never went anywhere or did anything without first consulting Jack.

For one thing, I could always count on Jack to tell me what I needed to know, not what I wanted to hear. He was famous for it. At the height of American despair at the way things were going in Vietnam, President Lyndon Johnson sent Jack to the jungle, instructing him to go everywhere, talk to everyone, and come back and tell him the truth about what was happening on the ground. After almost a month in Vietnam, Jack reported to the White House one day just after lunch while Johnson was taking his daily rest. Jack told the president that drugs in the forces were rampant, that our soldiers didn't understand why we were there, and that they were fragging their officers. "And the volunteers are all on the other side," Jack concluded. As Jack tells it, Johnson never opened his eyes. It was the last time Jack saw the president.

By way of briefing me on my new challenge, Jack once gave me a detailed description of the development of the South American drug trade and some of the ways it played out in Central America and Mexico as trans-shipment points en route to U.S. markets. The Reagan administration fought the ideological threat of advancing "communism" of Nicaragua's Sandinista movement by supplying a Honduran puppet army with hundreds of millions in military equipment. When the war ended, U.S. support dried up for Honduran generals, so they turned to the drug trade. "What do you think they're going to do?" concluded Jack. "Watch daytime television?"

In developing the Conservancy's International Program, we ultimately created a portfolio investment approach with a diverse array of risk and returns in a dozen countries from Mexico to Venezuela. In all of these countries, we supported local leadership and initiatives. Some worked better than others.

The Desert Sea, Mexico

High on my list from the get-go was Mexico—big, culturally and ecologically rich, and until recently, a country that maintained a refreshing independence from overbearing Americans to the north. I'd read *Distant Neighbors* by Alan Riding, former Latin American correspondent for the *New York Times*, who described Mexico as the most difficult country for the United States to penetrate and build relationships: Mexicans had too often been pushed around by the attitudes and self-serving intentions of Americans, to say nothing of having lost a big whack of their former empire from Texas to California to U.S. territorial expansion.

It didn't take me long in Mexico to see what Riding meant. I made it my first order of business to meet as many Mexican leaders as I could. These were men and women who, obviously, knew more about their home, not to mention about homegrown conservation, than I could ever hope to. And yet my assignment, from some Conservancy leaders' perspective, was to teach them what I knew about land preservation through private action. I felt vaguely as I had when at 15, people would ask me how I trained falcons to do what they do.

Also, my Peace Corps experience working with black Carib "Garifuna" fishermen on the north coast of Honduras had taught me something about the futility of trying to help the locals without first learning the local ways. So in the countless meetings I had with these Mexican leaders, I always stressed that what we wanted to do was to help local people solve their own problems in their own way in their own time. I vividly recall one of these leaders listening carefully to my pitch, then turning around and telling a compatriot that I was meeting with them because the Conservancy had more money than it knew what to do with and that I'd come to give some to those who would do as we said. It would take three to four years of dialogue before most Mexican leaders would begin to believe otherwise.

When I was scouting for leadership in Mexico, one of the Conservancy board members pointed me to Alejandro Garza LaGuerra, Chairman of DUMAC, Ducks Unlimited of Mexico, and a leading Mexican businessman. From modest beginnings one hundred years earlier, the Garza-LaGuerra families controlled huge Mexican business conglomerates from beer to steel to finance. I flew to Monterrey to meet Don Alejandro in 1981 and noticed an unusually large fleet of corporate jets at the airport. Don Alejandro was informally dressed, quietly cosmopolitan, gracious, and deeply committed to waterfowl conservation and wetland habitat restoration in northern Mexico, where millions of breeding North American waterfowl winter. Over a delicious dinner of local cuisine, he described DUMAC and asked if I would like to see some of their projects. He described a marshland restoration project in Chihuahua, suggested an early morning start to a daylong trip 800 miles or so to the west, and said he would invite the regional minister of agriculture to meet us for lunch. "How long will it take us to get there?" I asked. "About an hour and a half," Don Alejandro said. "We'll come back here for dinner to meet other conservationists in Monterey." That fleet of corporate airplanes was just part of the family empire.

When Don Alejandro understood that the Conservancy's deeper interest lay in biodiversity conservation rather than in improving duck habitat for hunters, he suggested I meet his cousin Andres Marcelo Sada, the chairman of another great Mexican business empire, Cydsa, and an avid birder. This I did on another trip to Monterrey and on later trips to his offices in the CitiBank Tower in the Zona Rosa of Mexico City. I had discovered one powerful, smart, strategic, generous, and committed conservationist. Don Andres had been a hunter like his cousins and enjoyed the out-of-doors. He was also, like most Mexicans, a devout Catholic. As he told it, his youngest child had fallen critically ill as an infant, and Don Andres promised the good Lord that if this child grew well, he would never hurt another living animal. And thus, he turned from bird hunting to bird watching and identified more species of Mexican birds than any other Mexican, living or dead. There was nothing that Don Andres would not do to help protect and restore habitat for Mexican birds.

Once, as we were discussing the challenges of addressing both conservation and development in places like Mexico, Don Andres said, "Lack of development is not a state of the economy. It is a state of mind. Societies do what societies think." This is something I've never forgotten.

Through all of these encounters I was also slowly learning where the power lay in land-use decisions in Mexico. To understand it, one has to go back to the Mexican Revolution of 1910, when peasants effectively overthrew large landed oligarchs and reconstituted land ownership mainly in the hands of small peasant communities called *ejidos*. Corporations were not allowed to own land, and private land ownership, even of smalls tracts, was the exception rather than the rule. While the government retained considerable control over what could and couldn't be done on vast areas of Mexican territory—say, logging, farming, or creating parks and protected areas—much of rural Mexico was controlled by *ejidos* and their *ejiditario* members. This meant that the decisions about conservation were driven by what contributed to the well-being of peasant communities—access to potable water, arable soil for small-scale farming, health services, and education.

This is not to say that all *ejidos* were providing great solutions to the needs of the rural Mexican populace. There were some remarkable local examples of conservation, development, and social well-being in some of the indigenous communities of Oaxaca and other traditional communities in remote parts of the country. On the other hand, there were relatively few examples of a development model ideally suited to a wide variety of Mexican geographic and cultural conditions.

One such hopeful example was brought to my attention by a German-Mexican social scientist named Helmut Janka. Helmut took me to Chetumal in Quintana Roo state in the heart of Mayan traditional territory on the Yucatan Peninsula. There we visited El Corozal, an *ejido* community where Helmut had helped develop the Plan Piloto Forestal. As the result of decades of careful collaborative research and initiative between the *ejiditarios* and Helmut's team, the *ejido* controlled a large area of seasonal dry tropical forest where community-based farming, forest management, a small sawmill, and furniture making was providing promising employment opportunities for members of the *ejido*. It was based on careful inventory and selective logging of native species such as mahogany and other valuable hardwood species, while maintaining the natural composition of the forest. Decisions about what and when to cut were left to community members based on their own information and on community needs, with the long-term health and well-being of both the forest and community members in mind.

Yet another hopeful example was emerging on the southern end of the development of Cancun: Bahía de Ascención, a vast inland bay surrounded by mangroves, grasslands, and scattered dry tropical forest and shrub. A lobstermen's co-op there had developed among local people both to limit the number of fishers and to protect small but robust populations of lobster and shellfish.

In addition to supporting Helmut's Plan Piloto, we helped create the UNESCO Sian Ka'an Man and the Biosphere Reserve, almost one million acres of land and sea around the Bahía de Ascención, where conservation and limited commercial and sport fishing, and tourism development, might continue to coexist. And we supported Amigos de Sian Ka'an, a Mexican independent organization that would continue to attempt to limit the incursions of large-scale tourism development to the north.

Yet another place in Mexico that appeared to have great promise was the Desert Sea, the magical Golfo de California—made famous by John Steinbeck in *The Sea of Cortez*. But here again we were faced with the challenge of developing a larger strategy in which conservation might succeed over the long term. How could we support local residents, the fishermen themselves, Baja California's two state governors, and federal officials in a long-range program to protect and restore the rich marine life of the Sea of Cortez? The Mexican government regulated the fishery, or not, as is the case with most governments around the world. As elsewhere, there were virtually no nongovernmental, nonprofit organizations devoted to conservation and community development in the Sea of Cortez. Government and industry was not accustomed to being challenged by an independent sector of civil society. The handful of committed conservationists in the Sea of Cortez worked for universities, research organizations, largely ineffective bureaucratic government institutions, or businesses.

Espíritu Santo, a newly protected island in Mexico's Sea of Cortez.

Tim Means aboard the *Don José*, in La Paz.

There were, however, people like Tim Means, who started Baja Expeditions based in La Paz, at the southern end of the thousand-mile-long Baja Peninsula, in 1974, after getting fired from Grand Canyon Expeditions. After a trip down the Colorado River, apparently, one of the two school buses transporting some 35 rafters home broke down, so they all piled into the other one, broke into a case of vodka, and Tim was arrested for mooning a state police officer while crossing Hoover Dam. Shortly thereafter he was unceremoniously thrown out of the Royal Las Vegas Hotel for leading a rather drunken party of rafters running naked through the lobby on their way to a quick skinny-dip in the pool. That happy ending concluded his 10 years of guiding on the Colorado, so Tim headed downstream to the river's mouth at the north end of the Sea of Cortez and just kept going south. Today, he runs some 35 trips a year for two thousand kayakers, birders, divers, and tourists of all ages out of La Paz: burro trips into the mountains of the interior, whale watching in San Ignacio Lagoon, and boat trips on the *Don Jose*—a 50-foot ship he built himself in La Paz—to the many isolated desert islands of the Sea of Cortez.

In the spring of 1982 Tim took a small team of Conservancy staff, board members, and supporters on a trip in the *Don Jose* to Isla Rasa and the surrounding Midriff Islands: a turquoise sea, white sandy beaches, high rocky hills, cactus, and desert shrub. On tiny Isla Rasa, 90 percent of the world's Elegant terns nest, a rare and delicate bird endemic to the region, along with Heerman's gulls and royal terns. One evening at sunset we visited a talus slope on the hillside above Cardinosa Beach to watch fish-eating bats depart from under their daytime roosts by the thousands, while Least and Black petrels returned by their thousands from their daytime open ocean fishing to their nests under the very same rocks. It was almost dark but the air was full of departing bats and arriving petrels. The next day, Bernardo Villa, the leading marine mammalogist in Mexico, and one of his students, Enriqueta Velarde, who had devoted her research life to protecting the island, walked us carefully around Isla Rasa amid the clamor of arriving and departing terns and gulls, while a Peregrine falcon sat nearby overlooking its young in an eyrie on a cliff 50 feet above the surrounding sea. Enriqueta and Dr. Villa were succeeding in fending off egg collectors from nearby coastal towns, and the birds were making a recovery to historic numbers. Eventually they succeeded in convincing the government to grant full protection to the islands, and their bird colonies are now at the center of a UNESCO Man and the Biosphere Reserve.

Our support of early efforts to gain protection for places like Isla Rasa and the greater Midriff Islands was eventually led by Alejandro Robles, a young Mexican marine biologist working out of Guaymas, on the mainland coast of the Sea of Cortez. He joined The Nature Conservancy International staff in 1985 and would become one of the early founders of Conservation International. Alejandro has been a force behind many successes of organizations like Niparaja, marine protected areas at Cabo Pulmo, and the protection of 35,000-acre Espíritu Santo Island. Known to his friends as "Waffles," Alejandro had a deep knowledge of both the natural history of the sea and relationships with local academic, scientific, and governmental institutions.

But our successes in Mexico were matched if not outnumbered by initiatives that didn't gain the support of local people and that were automatically and dogmatically opposed by fishermen and the Secretaria de Pesca. In some instances the government agreed to create new protected areas, but they were largely ineffective "paper parks" without local support or enforcement. It would not be until 2004, when Alejandro helped create a local organization Noroeste Sustenable, or "Nos," formed by local people to address both conservation and economic development, that a larger vision and strategy for the entire Sea of Cortez emerged. Fishermen are now supporting marine protected areas that they know will be a source for fishery recovery and renewal, places where they will defend and help enforce the no-fish regulations.

As the international staff at the Conservancy grew, we had long conversations trying to come up with an appropriate and powerful conceptual framework for conservation and development in Mexico. Our successes were by no means insignificant, but to take on the larger forces of social, economic, and environmental change, we needed much more powerful strategies. Land conservation by itself was necessary but altogether insufficient. Moreover, the Conservancy's particular brand of "land conservation through private action" was anathema in most of Mexico in the 1980s because, as noted above, private land ownership was limited and decisions were made by *ejidos* or government. In short, the Conservancy's model, however successful it might be in the States, had to be completely rethought in the international context. This seemed self-evident to those of us on the ground in Mexico and other parts of Latin America, but it was not always what the brass back home was prepared to hear. The Conservancy's uniquely American approach was clear, simple, and straightforward, and was becoming an enormous fundraising and conservation success: buy land and save it. The growing disparity between the culture of the mother ship and my own efforts to adapt to local circumstance should have given me more pause than it did, but I had my plate full trying to come up with ways to tap local energy and provide the social and economic benefits of conservation more broadly.

Beni, Bolivia

I first flew to the Beni River lowlands of Bolivia with Javier Castroviejo, the director of Spain's park service and the research program in the heart of the Coto Doñana in Seville, at the mouth of the Guadalquivir River. The Coto Doñana included the largest protected estuary and some of the last viable habitat in Europe for bobcats, imperial eagles, and abundant nesting and migratory waterfowl. Castroviejo, whom I'd originally met in Spain on a trip in 1984 with Conservancy board member Peter Stroh, had told me that The Nature Conservancy was on the wrong track in the Orinoco River flood forests, the *llanos* of Venezuela. There were even bigger, richer, and cheaper lands, he'd said, in the Beni River lowlands.

So Castroviejo and I headed off to Santa Cruz, in the eastern lowlands of Bolivia. One of Castroviejo's Bolivian rancher friends had shown up at the airport in a late-model white convertible Mercedes. It wasn't quite what I had visualized in this remote dusty frontier agricultural town, though I tried not to worry too much about the precise source of his apparent wealth. The lower Andean slopes from Santa Cruz to the Beni, the *yungas*, were ground zero for coca growers. The *cocaleros* farm coca plants, the popular and traditional leaf that has been chewed for centuries by indigenous people to elicit a soft high and stave off hunger. It is also, of course, the source of the paste from which cocaine is derived. Drug lords were prospering from here up the eastern flanks of the Andean cordillera all the way to Colombia.

From Santa Cruz we flew northwest for several hours, 20,000-foot Andean mountains towering out the left window and a seemingly endless, flat, and seasonally flooded Amazonian forest and savannah out the right one. It was the wild west, something an Oregon-born nature nut dreams about incessantly—what land conservation we could have done before everything went the way of development and degradation. Well, here it was. And land was cheap; six to eight dollars an acre struck a chord with the several enthusiastic ranchers we visited; 100,000 acres of jaguar and anaconda habitat for less than one million dollars.

We eventually settled on El Porvenir, a modest ranch of 5,000 acres. It had road access near the small frontier town of San Borja, served by intermittent airline connections to La Paz, and was an ideal location for an education and research station similar to Castroviejo's Coto Doñana model. Bolivian institutions committed to research, education, and conservation were in short supply in 1983. At that time there was only a nascent national system of parks and protected areas, and the nongovernmental sector was all but nonexistent. Everything depended on government, and after having had nearly more governments than years of republic, Bolivia was, let's say, thin on governmental capacity in even the most fundamental functions. But after months of discussions with Bolivian government agencies, international aid agencies, and independent organizations, the Academia de Ciencias Nacional de Bolivia emerged as an appropriate and enthusiastic partner in our adventures in the Beni. We shook hands with the owner of El Porvenir and headed home to Washington.

El Porvenir, a base for research, education, and tourism in the 300,000-acre national protected area, Estación Biológica del Beni.

But to officially close the deal, I needed more than a handshake; I needed a lawyer. Russ van Herik, a trial lawyer from the Midwest, had joined the Minnesota state office of The Nature Conservancy and worked his way up to midwestern regional vice president. He was very smart, soft-spoken but tenacious, and a skilled land negotiator. About this time, he admitted that he was losing interest in the challenges of land conservation in Iowa and wondered if he could be helpful in the International Program, even though he spoke no Spanish. It was a propitious moment—never mind the chasm between U.S. and Bolivian land tenure law, traditions, and behaviors. It wasn't long before Russ was on his way to Bolivia.

I don't remember all the details, but Russ's trip report upon returning to Washington a week or two later went something like this. He got off the plane at Bolivia's capital La Paz, elevation 12,000 feet in the altiplano of the Andes. He felt fine until he tried to pick up his suitcase, when he all but fell on the pavement from lack of air and exhaustion. Eventually he found a flight to San Borja on one of the venerable old twin propeller DC-3s, which so reliably served tropical country air service all over the developing world for 50 years or more.

Out the window, the mountains and forests stretched as far as Russ could see. Imagine his surprise when, instead of landing at the airport in San Borja, the plane set down on a rough dirt strip surrounded by cattle and cowboys. They threw open the large cargo doors, and the plane filled with hot humid air that made even Washington, D.C., in August feel temperate. The cowboys began slaughtering several cows destined for distant meat markets. No point in starting the butchering until the plane actually showed up, for such an arrival is altogether unpredictable in the Beni.

Russ was just beginning to get the international flavor of our work as big bloody sides of beef were tossed whole behind the passenger seats, followed by large flocks of flies. Then he noticed the pilot and engineer climbing a homemade ladder onto the wing and beginning to unbolt the left engine. It had been running rough, but not a problem; in the back country it's always good to have a spare engine in the cargo hold. With the help of a dozen or so cattle rustlers, barefoot young boys, and miscellaneous onlookers, and a hammer and rusty wrench, the new engine was successfully lifted up and bolted on. Several sweaty hours later, they were ready for the next stop in San Borja in a tropical downpour.

Russ's flight to the Beni was a foreshadowing of the succeeding negotiations, attempts to settle on precise terms and conditions for continued cattle grazing, allowing some of El

Porvenir's tenants to stay on, and then search for actual title, escrow accounts, and such. The Spanish-English translations might not have helped. But somehow Russ closed the deal and came home with something that looked sufficiently like a deed. Plus his letter of resignation. "I haven't the faintest bloody idea what you think we are doing in Bolivia!" We laughed. Iowa was looking pretty good after all.

Costa Rica

In contrast to Mexico, Bolivia, Brazil, and other large South American countries, Costa Rica was a relatively low-risk, low-return investment in terms of acreage of land conserved and total numbers of species protected. But it seemed worthwhile having some places of relatively "intensive" investment with solid, if not spectacular, returns, as an inspiration to other countries. Costa Rica was also a logical focus of early efforts of The Nature Conservancy International Program: a small country of remarkable biodiversity spanning both Atlantic and Pacific coasts, active volcanoes, and high mountains in the central cordillera with rich, moist, tropical rain forests on the Osa Peninsula; dry, seasonal forests in Guanacaste; and the lowland forests of the Atlantic. It is a relatively small country, modestly populated, deeply democratic, settled largely by Spanish, German, and Swiss farmers with a large number of small private land ownerships, coffee farms, truck farming on the rich volcanic soils of the central highlands, as well as banana plantations on the Caribbean slopes. Costa Rica also had the unusual early insight to dissolve its army and devote substantial public resources to education and, as a result, had one of the highest literacy rates in the world. It was a safe and relatively self-confident little country and was blessed with early leadership by a small cadre of remarkable individuals who committed the country to one of the strongest national systems of parks and protected areas in the world. These were the kinds of characteristics that led us to Costa Rica in the earliest days of The Nature Conservancy's adventures abroad.

"Us" at this point was Chuck Hedlund and myself. Chuck was a Conservancy board member who had retired at the early age of 63 from a worldwide career with Exxon in order to devote himself to international conservation. As unlikely as it might seem, this oilman and former chairman of the American Arabian Oil Company, Aramco, was a gentle farm boy from Minnesota at heart. Worldly wise, business smart, and, while ideologically shaped by his time and occupation, a completely committed conservationist who essentially devoted the rest of his life to our work.

Chuck and I visited Costa Rica in 1980 and quickly met some of the early pioneers of Costa Rican conservation, including Alvaro Ugalde, director of the government's Servicio de Parques Nacionales. Alvaro Ugalde's own journey toward "reliable prosperity" is one worth telling, and I can only hope that one day he will overcome his innate humility enough to tell it himself. Alvaro is a smart, no-nonsense, politically savvy, tenacious bulldog of a man who has dedicated his whole life to the conservation of Costa Rica's biodiversity. He grew up in San José, son of a highway department topographer who helped lay out many of Costa Rica's highways, with a devoted mother, a brother, and two sisters. He studied biology at the University of Costa Rica and soon after graduation was working as director of the budding Santa Rosa National Park. Alvaro is also a listener, deeply compassionate about the plight of ordinary Costa Ricans, on-and-off-again director of parks for more than 40 years, with stints with international organizations, and consulting assignments in distant places like Paraguay, Vietnam, and Guatemala.

As in Mexico, Costa Rican leaders knew what to do and just wanted our help to do it. Training programs aimed at making them more like North Americans were not on their agenda. They were building a national system of protected areas to preserve the full array of the country's natural heritage, and beginning to develop a nongovernmental sector, starting with the Fundacion de Parques Nacionales, a nonprofit designed to capture international funding for the park system. In 1982 he came to Washington, D.C., at my invitation to learn the nuanced art of hitting up gringos for large amounts of money. We launched a $6 million campaign for the National Parks of Costa Rica and hired a young Costa Rican woman named Liliana Madrigal to lead the effort. Liliana and Alvaro succeeded beyond our wildest dreams. Liliana herself became a legend in her own time and continues to this day to support indigenous communities and conservation throughout the Americas through her and her husband Mark Plotkin's Amazon Conservation Team.

Also of interest to Alvaro Ugalde and his colleagues was our methodology of biological inventory—what the Conservancy in the States called Natural Heritage Programs, and we in Latin America called Centros de Datos para la Conservacion (CDC). The Nature Conservancy's traditional biological inventory methods depended on knowledge about the full range of species and their habitats; in Costa Rica there were more species of plants and animals than in most of North America, relatively few of which were known, described, or mapped. Hence, mapping the sites of endangered species as a potential target for land conservation was an exercise in futility. Furthermore, time was of the essence. Bulldozers and chainsaws would not wait while we figured out exactly what species even existed.

A solution was found in Venezuela during our work with botanist Otto Huber from the Missouri Botanical Garden. Poring over early maps showing locations of endangered species "occurrences," our science director, Chilean biogeographer Guillermo Mann, and his Mexican-American sidekick, Martin Goebel, quickly realized all we really had was a map of roads, hotels, and scientific field stations—those relatively few places where scientists had traveled and studied. The rest of the map was blank; not because there weren't endangered species there, but rather because no one had looked yet. Huber and his colleagues, on the other hand, had, after many years of painstaking fieldwork, developed a national-scale map that described some 220 vegetation types, including their characteristic plant and animal species. So Guillermo and Martin used our emerging computerized geographic information system technology to overlay the map of existing national parks and protected areas on top of the Huber's vegetation map. Thus we discovered what sorts of ecosystems among Venezuela's incredibly diverse range of habitats were underrepresented in conserved lands. We were looking for gaps in the conservation portfolio—so-called gap analysis.

All the buzz was protecting tropical rain forests, but the first-cut gap analysis showed that a substantial part of Venezuela's tropical rain forests were already in protected status, while a very small percentage of savannah, dry thorn forests, and montane cloud forests were found in protected areas.

That this led to struggles with my old nemesis Bob Jenkins, VP for science, should come as no surprise. Like any good time-keeper, he insisted that the scientific methodology remain precisely the same everywhere, and that therefore the work of inventory should be the same in Venezuela as it was in Ohio. There are sound scientific reasons for this, of course, as well as less sound ones based on the overrated and tedious values of efficiency and consistency. With very few resources, and facing the pressure of losing species forever, we felt we had little choice.

Nor was Jenkins thrilled when our Costa Rican Centros de Datos para la Conservation was eventually absorbed by a new independent, nongovernmental organization called Instituto Nacional de Biodiversidad, or INBio, established in 1990. But the results were remarkable. Little did I imagine such a giant leap forward for our early, clumsy efforts at adapting a largely irrelevant methodology from the United States.

Take the case of Elena Ulate, an untrained young woman who did what few of our own overeducated experts could imagine. Now in her mid-30s, Elena works for INBio and stares into a microscope sorting tropical beetles into family, genera, and species. She has been doing this since she was 15. There are an estimated 335,000 insect species, of which perhaps only 10 percent have been described by science, in her native Costa Rica. Elena's task is a difficult one. She is one of maybe 10 people in the world who can distinguish different species of beetle in Costa Rica. She barcodes every species and is helping build a national biodiversity collection unlike any in the world.

INBio, which has grown into a prestigious international organization with hundreds of staff and a multimillion-dollar budget, was created by Rodrigo Gámez, one of the small cadre of conservationists with whom I worked in the early 1980s to protect the fast-diminishing 20 percent of the country still untouched by logging, agricultural development, and ranching. INBio's jump-start in inventory began when it assumed responsibility for the Costa Rican Centro de Datos para la Conservacion we had built in the early 1980s.

We also worked with the Servicio de Parques Nacionales to develop a strategy for the fast-increasing interest in ecotourism. I remember a strategy meeting about ecotourism in San José with Alvaro Ugalde and his colleagues, along with my hero Jack Vaughn. Research had revealed that tourism could become the leading economic sector of the country, ahead of agriculture, if we could entice ecotourists to stay just one more day in the country. "That'll be easy," said Jack. "Just be sure they fly Lacsa," the national airline famous for leaving desperate passengers stranded for hours, and sometimes days, waiting for a flight home.

Elena Ulate Arce, at INBio's scientific collections in San José.

It was a bit harder than that, of course, but today ecotourism is easily leading the country's economy, and unfortunately, it threatens the park system itself with the encroaching eco-hungry. Little did we imagine that success with the park system would lead to international

Dr. Rodrigo Gámez, president of INBio in San José, Costa Rica.

airports in once-dusty cattle country with direct flights to Toronto, Miami, New York, and Dallas. A Costa Rica enthusiast in LA can now leave the office just a little early on Friday and be home for lunch on Monday after a weekend on the beaches of Costa Rica's northwest Guanacaste coast. There's probably not an unprotected beach on the Pacific that doesn't have an eager developer planning a new "eco-resort." True to its name, Costa Rica's coastal land values have increased 50 to 60 fold since Alvaro Ulgade and others acquired large parts of the Guanacaste coast in the early 1980s for national parks. Another reminder of the pitfalls in the department of "be careful what you wish for."

Today, Alvaro Ulgade is devoted to the restoration of a few small watersheds in north-central Costa Rica. But this time it isn't the acreage of reforestation or the amount of funding that concerns him. Today it's the how, not the what—specifically, how does one help release the energy of local people, acting in their own self-interest, to drive the metabolism of the environmental movement? What might a truly bottom-up, grassroots movement look like, and what is the spark, the catalyst, necessary to make

Cache: *Creating Natural Economies*

Alvaro Ugalde has been a mainstay of conservation in Costa Rica for over 40 years.

it happen? After a lifetime of fighting to remove gold miners and hunters from places like Parque Nacional de Corcovado to prevent adjacent development, Alvaro discovered that all of Costa Rica is organized by law into watershed associations in which the adult members of the community, men and women, have responsibility for the quality and quantity of their water supply. While many of the headwaters of watersheds in Costa Rica are protected in national parks, the grazing, logging, farming, and urban development in the lower parts now threaten many communities' water supply. Quite simply, without an intact watershed, people have no water, or too little, or it is too dirty or too unreliably available. Alvaro discovered many small communities where the women are taking the initiative to defend and restore their watersheds. So he created a small revolving eco-loan fund from which watershed associations can borrow money at zero percent financing but 100 percent ecological interest to acquire degraded land and, with modest amounts of technical support, remove the cattle, repair the fences, raise native tree seedlings in nurseries, and replant the hillsides. He spends his time visiting the women in the associations, working with school children in elementary schools, and providing what modest advice and encouragement he can—a small loan, some help selecting the right tree species, and planting techniques and guidance that they request. That's all. And he has unleashed a whole new movement.

What's Alvaro's take-home message from all this? The key to both development and conservation is releasing the energy of local residents. The one powerful force that is growing in a world of increasing scarcity is the unlimited creativity of human imagination when addressing its own perception of self-interest.

I don't pretend that I understood this with anything like clarity in the late 1980s, but what I did understand was that The Nature Conservancy's approach of private land conservation was inadequate to the task at hand in Latin America. Ultimately we would either have to change the culture, the board, and the staff of The Nature Conservancy to become truly international, or develop a subsidiary or related entity that could grow from the Conservancy's great history and reputation to take on the task of conservation and development in ways that would have enduring effect. Neither option would be easy to pull off.

71

4

CREATION MYTH: *High Drama in D.C.*

So back to the Tabard Inn and Conservation International's creation myth. By now you have some idea of the conflicts involved and the outcomes at stake. It's time to recount the immediate events that led to what was as much an uprising as a resignation. Janie and I had moved back to Portland in 1984, yearning to be closer to friends and family—home—and I had been trying to turn The Nature Conservancy's international work over to Peter Seligmann. Then, in January of 1987, all hell broke loose.

Undeniably, The Nature Conservancy faced an intriguing organizational challenge—to give the International Program the freedom and flexibility it needed to succeed while maintaining the integrity of a single organization with a long and successful history in the U.S. of A. This had become a key strategic planning issue for the organization for several years after it was clear that we had contributions to make around the world. Five of the Conservancy's key board members and important donors were on the international committee. Chuck Hedlund, our closest friend and ally, had been chairman of the Conservancy's board. Ambassador Jack Vaughn chaired the volunteer committee, and

Peter Stroh chaired the international committee. Jean Vollum was by then on the board as well as my close friend Sophie Engelhard Craighead, by then married to none other than John Craighead's eldest son, Derek.

Pete Seligmann and I had argued that the Conservancy's mission was biodiversity conservation: the vast majority of Earth's biodiversity resides in the developing tropics, so the organization should be international in mission, composition, and structure. I thought that under Pete's leadership, I could step back with succession well established—a great team of some 60 mostly Latin American women, and a plan for the development of the International Program well underway. Pete and I thought we had a clear understanding of the relationship between the national headquarters and the International Program that allowed us to succeed while maintaining cooperation, collaboration, and synergy with the Conservancy's state and national programs. And Frank Boren, a good friend of ours and father of one of our best staff members, was coming to Washington to replace Bill Blair as the new president of the Conservancy and had made it clear he just wanted to turn us loose. "You have the A Team, I have the B Team. I just want you to run," Frank said.

However, when I sketched it out on a napkin for Bill Blair, the Conservancy's president at the time, a light about what we really had in mind finally went on for him. It showed an international board composed of people from the countries around the world in which we worked, an international staff composed of professionals from their respective countries, mostly located in-country, and policies and programs that were culturally and technically designed to address the enormous challenges involved in promoting a global agenda of conservation and development. Under the president were vice presidents for the United States, Latin America, Asia, and Africa. To be effective, it was not to be a U.S. show with Americans running around the world training everyone to become like us. Quite the contrary. Residents of the countries and communities where we worked would teach us how we could help. We had demonstrated that conservation by itself was simply insufficient in countries where there really was no "wilderness" empty of human influence, indigenous or otherwise, where expanding populations of rural poor lived on and by the land, where heat and cooking fuel came from wood from nearby forests, potable (or not) water from streams, and subsistence food from the land. To succeed we would have to help local people solve their own problems in their own way. Ignoring their principal social and economic needs would result in no conservation, more poverty, and little true economic development.

That napkin turned Bill Blair's world upside down. Despite, or perhaps because of, his many years in public affairs at the U.S. Department of State, he hadn't understood what we had been arguing for months—that the U.S.A. had to be part of a global institution rather than on top of it. Our picture of an ideally structured, truly international program threatened every existing power relationship in the organization. Many of the Conservancy's more traditional American board and staff simply could not imagine how to rethink the Conservancy in these terms. It had a 40-year history in the United States, led the movement of "land conservation through private action," and was funded entirely by U.S. donors. The state chapters wouldn't have it. Competition for major donors would be everywhere. Bill and many of our colleagues could only imagine a strong and powerful U.S. organization with an "international program" at its side, very much the traditional American view of the world—an initiative that Americans with their infinite wisdom and wealth could control, one that was designed to serve a large, successful American organization's self-interest. It's a model that, not incidentally, pretty much parallels the industrial-model relationship of humans to the rest of the natural world.

Pete, our board members, and I were well aware it might be too big a transition for the Conservancy. So we didn't insist it be completely reorganized from the get-go, but argued instead for sufficient independence to develop an international board, science, communications, development staff, and donors to serve the international initiatives. We suggested a 509(a), a nonprofit analog to a wholly owned subsidiary organization, and had Conservancy friend and counsel William T. Hutton draft by-laws and incorporation papers. It would give the international program its own structure while resting it within the parent organization's ultimate control (the parent would elect board members and could fire them and the staff if necessary). But after months of haggling with the bureaucracy, we decided in the spring of 1986 to experiment for a year with the 509(a) international structure in the form of "chapter" status, with essentially the same, but less formal, arrangements. Pete and I thought we were finally free to spend our energies on the work at hand. The Latin American staff were elated and we went into overdrive.

The whole struggle has repeated itself so many times in so many forms through history that we must have been extremely naive to not understand the difficulties we faced. George W. Bush's Iraq and even President Obama's Afghanistan adventures are recent examples of the same America-centric view of the world, but it's been the MO of imperial power through history. It's the way the U.S. government behaves across the board and around the world. Churches do it; corporations do it. Indeed, in an ecological sense, all organisms fight first for their own survival and ability to reproduce, everything else being secondary. And the search for food defines natural relationships, so the donor-nonprofit relationship demands results in simple terms—none of this wishy-washy capacity-building in some obscure indigenous village whose name no one can pronounce. Perhaps in our idealism in the nonprofit do-good world, we thought it would all work out happily.

It didn't. Frank Boren—a Harvard-trained football player, attorney, and no-nonsense, get-the-job-done board member of the California Chapter of The Nature Conservancy—thought he would come to town, turn us loose, and focus on building the U.S. programs. Little did he know. When he got to the national office, he found some of the key senior staff livid that the International Program was on its own course, cultivating major new donors, building its own style of science programs, initiating conversations in China, and communicating with the national staff as equals rather than suplicants. Frank found he either had to get the International Program under control or lose the confidence of some of his senior staff. One wise board member told him he had a choice between "heart attack or cancer." Heart attack was getting us under control at the risk of losing key staff; cancer was not doing so and gradually losing control of the future of the organization and key donor relationships. In my conversations with Frank on the West Coast, I told him that if he tried to bring the whole Latin American staff under Washington control, the very qualities that made the program so successful would be threatened and most of the staff might resign. That was a mistake; his reaction was to insist that we all sign a loyalty oath. Unfortunately, in his secret conversations with Peter Stroh and some of the international board members, he made a big deal of his loyalty oath. Stroh had done his masters thesis on Hitler Germany's oath of loyalty, and his antennae went straight up. Chuck Hedlund told us that Frank was on a mission to divide and conquer. In mid-January 1987, I flew once again to Washington and checked into the Tabard Inn to see what might be done.

It was a mess. Frank would spend time with us at the old International Program office on Massachusetts Avenue and agree we were on the right track. Then he would go back across the Key Bridge on the Potomac to Conservancy headquarters in Arlington, and Bob Jenkins and the national staff would convince him he had to cut us off at the knees.

Frank Boren wanted me to work directly for him. Henry Little was still on the International Program staff but was secretly telling Boren everything. Geoff Barnard, who had helped develop our Costa Rica programs, was trying to mediate the whole thing while negotiating with Frank about taking over leadership of the International Program, if and when Pete was fired. The Latin American staff were completely distraught at the prospect of losing their hard-won independence. Frank Boren's daughter Ashley, who worked for us in the International Program raising money for the Charles Darwin Foundation in the Galapagos Islands, was clearly torn between her professional and family loyalties; she eventually quit and went back home to California to pursue an MBA at Stanford.

Hedlund, former chair of the Conservancy's board and a key supporter of the International Program, and Stroh, chair of the Conservancy board's International Committee, were trying to get Frank back under control. Stroh came to Washington and took the Conservancy Chairman Jon Roush, Frank Boren, and John Flicker, its executive vice-president, and me to dinner at a little French restaurant called Tout Va Bien.

Tout did not *va bien* that dark wintry night in Georgetown. Stroh realized headquarters staff were telling him one thing while doing something else. Jon Roush was on the fence, but Frank Boren was pounding the table defensively, saying the Conservancy was run by staff and he would make the decisions regardless of what the board thought. About midnight the maitre d' tried to tell us the restaurant was closing. Normally the most gentle and kindly man I knew, a red-faced Peter Stroh demanded more drinks and said he would buy the place if necessary to finish the conversation. The conversation ended in a stalemate, and Stroh was furious.

Later, Jack Vaughn, Hedlund, and Stroh made one more run at Frank, but reluctantly agreed that if they were unsuccessful they would help us start a new organization to keep the team together. Vaughn was serving as the Conservancy's volunteer committee chair but was always wise counsel. He said that a national office takeover of the International Program was the same old American pattern of imperialism. "It'll never work, no matter how you try to finesse it," Jack counseled. "I've seen the story unfold over and over. They leave you alone when you're struggling. When you create a success they take over and botch it every time."

Our international staff, particularly an extraordinarily strong team of Latin American women, couldn't wait for the revolution. The problem was, of course, money. We couldn't ask the staff to work for free—they had moved from distant countries, families and all. They had kids in school, mortgages, car loans, and doctor's bills to pay. We'd have to find long-term sources for the millions of dollars that comprised salary and benefits and programs—and right away, or the whole show would unravel as quickly as we could create it.

Nonetheless, Pete and I decided to go for it. We couldn't sacrifice the very principles that made the team and the work successful by kowtowing to colleagues who didn't seem to understand what we had to deal with in Latin America. The international staff couldn't wait. And so on January 26, 1987, I sat at a desk at the Tabard Inn and drafted a letter of resignation. We asked Bill Hutton to incorporate Conservation International the next day in California, using the same by-laws and articles of incorporation we had originally drafted to create a 509(a) subsidiary of The Nature Conservancy.

Somewhere in the chaos someone noticed that our office lease with the National Trust for Historic Preservation would expire in a few days. Rodolfo Flores, our International Program finance director, called the Trust and asked them to rewrite the lease in the name of Conservation International. Unfortunately, they called the Conservancy's National Office to confirm the name in the new lease. John Flicker was, appropriately, furious and fired Rodolfo the next day. Rodolfo was the only one of the renegade bunch who, in the end, actually got fired.

Meanwhile, rumblings of discontent between national and international forces at the Conservancy were beginning to leak out. Murray Gell-Mann, chair of the World Resources and Environment Program of the MacArthur Foundation in Chicago—a gold mine for both international and domestic programs of the Conservancy—stopped by Bob Jenkins' office in late January of 1987 on his way to a physics symposium in Baltimore and asked what was going on. Besides being a Nobel Prize–winning physicist, Murray was also an avid bird watcher and had traveled extensively with us all over Latin America, so he knew and liked the staff, especially some of the gorgeous Latin

American women. On hearing what was going on, Murray told Jenkins that he thought many of the international staff would resign if their independence was threatened. Jenkins made a $1,000 bet that not more than a handful of staff would leave. Murray said he couldn't take his money. They reduced the bet to a case of their favorite beer.

On January 30, 1987, Pete and I delivered the letter of resignation that 35 staff had signed, with more departures of both staff and board on their way. Eventually 55 of the 63 international staff, fellows, and interns left, along with five prominent board members. The Conservancy's former chairman, Chuck Hedlund, resigned, along with Peter Stroh, chairman of the international committee, and Jack Hood Vaughn, chairman of the volunteer committee. We had a big party with Colombian staff member Raquel Gomez's boyfriend's band and danced all night to celebrate.

I rented another room at the Tabard Inn and we prepared for CI's first board meeting. Someone was coming up the stairs with food and drinks and said a familiar-looking person was sitting quietly in a chair in the lobby watching. I went down and found Murray Gell-Mann, who'd won his case of beer from Bob Jenkins.

"I heard what happened," he said, "and just wanted to be close by."

"My God, Murray," I said. "Come up and join us!" The staff were all in tears as he came in the room.

Jack Vaughn followed close on his heels. *"Abajo la rosca, vive la revolucion!"* he shouted. Jack, Chuck, Peter Stroh, and a few other unsuspecting witnesses were elected to the board, and we voted in articles and by-laws. Conservation International was born on Janie's birthday, January 30, 1987.

We didn't have an office, credit cards, phone, or rolodexes. The Conservancy put a security guard on our old offices at the National Trust building. They threatened to put us all in jail for stealing donors, technology, and intellectual property, and launched a publicity campaign with the remaining board and donors. Janie and I put our Portland home in her name. CI hired Charlie Steele, a Harvard-trained lawyer friend in Washington who had won Supreme Court decisions. The Conservancy sent staff to my Portland office to take my computer hard drives to prove their case that it had all been a conspiracy. There was no such thing of course, but it was chaos. It was a somber Monday morning when the realization sank in that we were in fact no longer The Nature Conservancy International and would have to start fresh. I'd had no idea what real stress felt like. The sense of insecurity and responsibility for all these wonderful people, the work in-country, the reputations and well-being of all concerned, including the Conservancy, was all but overwhelming.

Somehow we didn't miss a day of salary. I had hit the road for several days and rounded up over $4 million in commitments from some of our most trusted individual donors to keep the team together. Pete worked on his supporters. It was some 55 of us scattered from Washington to Portland to Bolivia that started CI, driven in many ways by the fierce loyalty to principles of local sovereignty on the part of leading revolutionary Latin American men and women. Ken Margolis, my old mentor and colleague, called from Costa Rica, where he was trying to check himself and some important donors into the Mariposa Hotel high on a hill overlooking Manual Antonio Park. "My credit card doesn't work!" Margolis said.

"That's because we quit and started CI!"

"Well, save me a space. I'd rather sink with you guys than swim with the ones on the other side of the Potomac!"

In the midst of all this, I was getting calls from the *Wall Street Journal*, and studiously ignoring them. I had heard the *Journal* was investigating dissension in the environmental movement. I could understand the press's interest in the story of a revolution within a major environmental organization, but I was just too busy to deal with it. Also, I was torn: on the one hand, the last thing I wanted was to pour fuel on the fire and bring the Conservancy down on us even harder; on the other hand, I didn't want the story to be published without getting an honest view of our side of things. Finally, after about the fourth of these calls I decided I had to take it.

"Hello," I said, preparing my thoughts. "Yes, this is Spencer Beebe."

"Ah," said the voice from the other end, "This is the *Wall Street Journal* calling and we were wondering if you're aware that your subscription is about to lapse and wanted to know if you will renew."

So much for high drama in the international conservation movement.

5

BOLIVIA: *A First and Last Hurrah*

Conservation International came into being January 30, 1987. By June of that year, the prospects for its survival were dicey at best. A revolution within the revolution was well underway. Both funding and tempers were running short, and we were all feeling pretty desperate. Paul Hawken, perhaps the world's most articulate spokesman for sustainability, joined our board and made a valiant effort with staff to prevent a complete meltdown. But we needed a big success in the field to get us off the ground, and we knew it. We found it in Bolivia.

The Beni, Revisted

I still thought of Bolivia as a place where we could make a big difference for relatively little money—something in very short supply at Conservation International. I also liked what our Conservancy project in the Beni River lowlands represented, a seeding of local scientific efforts. It was a bottom-up approach of sorts. Of course, most importantly, it was a trove of biodiversity located in the Amazon basin and within a corridor from the mountains to the lowlands, a swath of land home to 500 mammals and 1,000 species of birds.

When I was with The Nature Conservancy, we'd looked for new ways to leverage the value of U.S. dollars to support programs in more than a dozen Latin American countries. We explored "blocked" currencies—profits from multinational corporations that local laws prevented from being repatriated to headquarters outside the country. We made the case to a number of companies that they could do well and do good, after taxes, by donating the in-country blocked funds for our conservation work in those countries. It didn't fly. Financial crises were peaking in virtually all Latin American countries, and most were unable to service foreign debt. The annual inflation rate in Bolivia was running at more than 2,000 percent. Latin American debt was trading at 10 to 50 percent of face value, and prospects were bleak that countries would be able to repay their loans to international banks, foreign governments, and multilateral agencies like the World Bank.

Not only was this bad for the institutions making the loans, it was bad for the nations holding the loans. Rather than fostering local economies, whatever cash the debtor nations had on

Agricultural development is quickly eroding vast areas of tropical rain forests in Bolivia's Amazonian lowlands.

hand was leaving the country in order to service interest on the loans, compounding their need for foreign cash. Worse, the only way most Latin American nations could repay their loans was to accelerate harvest of their natural resources—trees and minerals—a bad situation for conservation and biodiversity.

When the debt crisis hit, we began to explore acquiring sovereign debt at the market's increasingly deep discounts with the hopes of trading it with the respective countrys' central banks for local currency and local commitments to conservation. It was a novel idea, a way to preserve land and slow resource extraction. But most of the board and senior staff at the Conservancy had been far too entrenched in their traditional cash-for-lands approach to approve something so radical.

At virtually our first board meeting at Conservation International, however, the idea was hailed. When we floated it, Alan Weeden, one of our founding board members, said, "I'll buy that," and donated $100,000 to the effort. Next, I went to see Bill Spencer, a senior executive at CitiBank. There was a market for foreign debt—buy at 10 cents and sell for 12 cents. CitiBank located a Swiss Bank that was willing to take our $100,000 for a $650,000 Bolivian central bank debt note. The Swiss Bank had given up expecting ever to be repaid because of the financial crisis.

Then, Guillermo Mann and Maria Teresa Ortiz, our Bolivian program leadership, went to the Banco Nacional de Bolivia and made our pitch: "You owe Conservation International $650,000 USD," they said. "But let's talk." They proposed to tear up the note if the bank would give $500,000 in Bolivian pesos to their own Academia de Ciencias Nacional to endow their program of research and education at El Porvenir. They asked that Bolivia create a UNESCO Man and the Biosphere Reserve, protecting the 300,000-acre Estacion Biologica del Beni, pristine forest surrounding the research station, and supporting conservation and ecological development in a huge surrounding areas. It would be an assemblage of conservation and development lands exceeding 1.2 million hectares, almost three million acres, from montane cloud forests to the Amazonian flood forests and savannah

of the Beni. The central bank accepted. Not only did they save
$150,000 off the top of the note, but they avoided having to make
the $500,000 payment in "hard currency" U.S. dollars, some-
thing that, with their rapid inflation and scarcity of funds, they
didn't have. But within Bolivia, the pesos worked just fine to
fund their own programs. The deal was done. In July 1987, just
months after its creation, Conservation International completed
the first "debt-for-nature swap" in the world.

The freedom that CI gave us to explore and innovate without the constraints of traditional thinking allowed us to quickly
explore a mechanism to reverse the downward spiral of interde-
pendent environmental and financial deterioration. We helped
reduce the country's debt burden. By funding the Academia de
Ciencias in local currency, something the government wished to
do in any event as part of their ongoing commitment to a national
program of science by distinguished Bolivian scientists, we helped
a sovereign organization carry out their field research in the Beni,
establish a long-term presence in the region, and build relationships with local, national, and international organizations.

Beni River llanos, Bolivia—seasonally flooded Amazonian lowlands.

As an endowment, the debt-for-nature swap brought continuity and put energy behind their programs on the ground, while for the first time in their long history also putting them on the global map. It created a permanent protected area, the first of its kind in Bolivia, of almost 300,000 acres around the field station, thus assuring scientists that their work would never be lost to deforestation. And by gaining the commitment of the government to support long-term conservation and appropriate development for indigenous people like the Chimane Indians and rural peasant populations in the region, we were encouraging a bottom-up approach to community-based "sustainable" development. And we created a new mechanism to vastly expand financial resources for conservation in the developing tropics worldwide—swapping debt for nature.

The international press went crazy. How could a conservation organization that no one had heard of come up with a tangible mechanism to help solve a global financial crisis? We were on the front page of the *Wall Street Journal* and featured in the *Economist* magazine, then hundreds of newspaper and magazine articles worldwide. Dozens of academic papers appeared within months. I was invited to spend a week in Japan with the Ministry of Finance. A whole series of debt-for-nature swaps—ultimately over $1 billion—unfolded from Madagascar to Mexico. Costa Rica did a series of debt-for-nature swaps that funded conservation programs and organizations like INBio for decades. Harvard did a debt-for-education swap in Ecuador. The Nature Conservancy, World Wildlife Fund, and many others eventually got into the game. The momentum continued for almost 20 years around the world. By 2008, Bolivia had virtually no foreign debt, President Evo Morales' cozy relationship with socialism and Venezuela President Chavez notwithstanding. The Bolivian debt-for-nature swap put Conservation International on the map; we were at last a viable and credible organization, capable of executing a kind of creativity that had become difficult at The Nature Conservancy. The MacArthur Foundation shortly approved a $3 million grant to CI for general support.

But the devil is indeed in the details. Bolivian politicians of the opposite party criticized the Minister of Agriculture for "giving its sovereign natural resources to foreigners." Throwing a gringo in the sea has always been Latin American politicians' favorite indoor sport—often, of course, with justification. Anthropologists denounced CI as another imperial opportunist for ignoring the interests of indigenous people. In fact, the amount of Bolivian staff and financial resources available to us to do the long-term, community-based, bottom-up job was inadequate. Harvesting of the biggest and best mahogany trees from the tropical forests continued unabated. El Porvenir's location was not as strategic as we hoped. We had leveraged some important work with global implications, but, as usual, it was anything but perfect.

Looking Back, Going Forward

In interviews 20 years after CI's original debt-for-nature swap, virtually every Bolivian I spoke with who had been involved said the swap created new resources unimaginable previously and helped to jump-start the whole Bolivian conservation movement. By 2008, the park system included 22 areas encompassing more than 20 percent of the country. But they were also conscious that developing the system so quickly with mostly foreign support pushed a preservationist agenda ahead of social development designed to address the legitimate needs of growing populations of rural poor. By 2008, the Bolivian government provided only a small percent of the $7 million annual budget of the park system, testament to the true priorities of political leadership in the country today.

Instead, over the past 20 years, in recognition of its enormous size, invaluable biodiversity, and growing system of protected areas, Bolivia has received extraordinary support from a wide range of bilateral and multilateral agencies, including USAID, the World Bank, and the Dutch, Swiss, German, and Spanish governments. Conservation International has a talented and completely Bolivian staff of 20 to 30, including several indigenous people,

Jorge Añez Claros, president of the Gran Consejo de Chimanes. San Borja, Bolivia 2009.

with a homey little office in La Paz and an annual budget in excess of $3 million. The Nature Conservancy and World Wildlife Fund now have similar staffs and budgets. CI has worked collaboratively with numerous Bolivian and international organizations to publish a wide range of scientific and educational material, and help save millions of acres of threatened tropical rain forests while promoting rational development.

But a telling sign of the times is that CI periodically removes its sign from the door, depending on changing public sentiment and national politics. Dr. Olvidio Suarez passed away and the Academia de Ciencias lost interest in and funding for the El Porvenir research station in the late 1990s. In the summer of 2008, a wildfire swept through neighboring grassland and burned some of the key facilities to the ground. The fences have fallen down, and neighboring cattle make good use of its abundant and free forage. The Academia is offering to convey title to the national park service. Local ranchers are still unconvinced. "Cattle earn money for me," said one influential rancher during meetings with municipal officials in San Borja. "Jaguars eat cattle. So I shoot jaguars." Jorge Añez Claros, who represents 15,000 Chimane Indians in 120 communities in and around the Estacion Biologica del Beni (EBB) told me that the Chimane still lack basic social services and facilities, are growing in numbers, and still live at the edge of subsistence.

Meanwhile, a single Movima Indian park guard watches over the ruins at El Porvenir with funds barely sufficient to feed his wife and son. But wood storks, black jaguarundi, fox, and black caiman abound, and large flocks of parrots of a dozen species and the orange billed toucan, park symbol of the Estacion Biologica del Beni, still find abundant food in native fruit trees.

El Porvenir, a 5,000-acre biological field station near San Borja, Bolivia.

Anacondas are doing fine. Occasionally, some unsuspecting adventurers with an out-of-date *Lonely Planet* find their way to El Porvenir hoping to get closer to nature. And they do.

Clearly, however, this is not what CI originally envisioned. Our thought was to build local capacity for "ecosystem-based management and people-centered solutions." Relying on large international organizations with local capacity—i.e., local staff of nationals—is different than building autonomous local capacity. It's the latter that is needed and that enables local people to find local solutions. Smart strategy needed to know when to enter and when to leave—something CI sometimes struggled to get right.

During a visit to La Paz, Mexico, in early 2009, I spoke to Alejandro Robles about this. After I'd originally hired Alejandro in 1988, he was promoted to a CI vice president in charge of Mexico programs, then moved to Washington to run the Mexico and Central America programs from headquarters. He said that this peak of his professional advancement was when he felt most powerless, least effective, and most eager to return home. There is a great sense of power for a Mexican like Alejandro to be part of a big international organization, live in Washington, D.C.,

Remnants of a building fire at El Porvenir in 2008.

have a well-equipped office, participate in senior staff meetings and board meetings with billionaire donors and "captains of industry," and raise funds to support local initiatives. It makes it very difficult to leave. CI has a lot of very effective people in biologically important places doing critical work, but sometimes it seems to have been just too incomprehensibly difficult to develop local capacity in the ways we had originally imagined. Where there is a big successful project, the donors all want to be part of it. As Alejandro put it, "They want to buy output from above. But when times are most difficult, when help is most needed, the large donors all want to be elsewhere." This is symptomatic of a recurring paternalistic relationship that makes building sustained local capacity particularly difficult. Alejandro felt trapped in a place in which he couldn't succeed, but couldn't leave.

As for me, I left Conservation International in February of 1991. It had been a strenuous few years. I'd moved back to Portland long before, in late 1984, tired of Washington, D.C., and tired of the international flights. I wanted to stay closer to home with Janie and the kids and my aging mother and father.

In 1989, several key World Wildlife Fund staff, including Russ Mittermeier, joined CI. Pete and Russ rebuilt a team loyal to their emerging strategies around tropical "hotspots" of biodiversity and more traditional biodiversity preservation. Many of the original staff left. By 1990, it seemed clear that a new and different CI was arising, and that my priorities lay in the rain forests of the Pacific Northwest. I began to look at temperate rain forests and the ways in which we might translate back to English at home some of the lessons learned abroad in tropical rain forest conservation and development. "If rain forests are so important, and sustainable development is all the buzz," I asked myself, "why not explore sustainable development in our own rain forests?" It was an amicable, natural, and productive evolution.

Today CI works in some 40 countries around the tropical world, has a prominent and truly international board of directors, 1,500 staff (most of whom are nationals of the countries in which they work), a $239 million 2008 budget, and has helped preserve millions and millions of acres of hotspot tropical lands. Like all organizations, it has taken on the personalities of its leadership—Russ Mittermeier and Peter Seligmann. It is by any measure far more successful than anything I might have imagined when I jumped ship on The Nature Conservancy. Thomas Friedman, the *New York Times* columnist and author of *Hot, Flat and Crowded*, gives CI credit for his education about biodiversity and the urgent need for a modern conservation ethic. His wife Ann is on the CI board, and he travels widely with CI staff and describes how the world needs a million Noahs (local leaders) and a million arks (regional conservation areas). In an April 12, 2009, editorial he cites a visit to Costa Rica with CI's regional vice president Carlos Manuel Rodriguez and touts Costa Rica's remarkable leadership in conservation, payments for ecosystem services, and its decision not to drill for oil, but rather to increase its proportional reliance on renewable energy.

There are also whole books written about CI and the other "BINGOs"—big international nongovernmental (environmental) organizations—criticizing them for the same imperial arrogance that inspired us to leave The Nature Conservancy in January 1987. Frankly, I'm not sure what the truth is. Perhaps I just don't want to know or prefer to believe all the good stuff and ignore the gory details that inevitably unfold. I have my own quota of foolish naiveté or ignorance, and my own selfish myths like those that haunt the true stories of Noahs everywhere.

INTERLUDE

6

APPRENTICESHIPS REVISITED

"In the middle of the journey of my life
I found myself astray in a dark wood
where the straight road had been lost sight of."
—Dante, *The Divine Comedy*

Well, "astray in a dark wood" is a bit overdramatic for where I found myself in that February of 1991, but the straight road, insofar as I'd tried to follow it at all, had definitely been lost sight of. I'd given my all to The Nature Conservancy and had brazenly tried to blaze a new trail with Conservation International, and, to say the least, things hadn't turned out exactly as I'd planned. If I was going to go forward—and I seem to have been born lacking a reverse or even a neutral gear—I needed to take stock of what had gone wrong. Or, at least, I needed to get in touch with what had started me off on this journey in the first place.

Though I hadn't consciously entertained the idea of starting yet another organization, I had fairly definite notions of what I would try to avoid should it come to that. Looking back, it seems clear to me now that the values I've tried to instill in the culture of Ecotrust are ones that I'd learned long before I joined up with The Nature Conservancy. I don't mean to sound ungrateful for the invaluable experiences that

95

the Conservancy and CI afforded me. But much of what I learned from those experiences had to do with the limitations of bureaucratic thinking even when exercised in the service of causes I enthusiastically endorsed. I knew there had to be a better way; I just had to remember what it was. Something to do with birds . . . and bananas . . . and a boat.

Learning from Birds

I don't know how my parents did it. They'd somehow load up the '52 Chevy station wagon with five screaming kids and a dog or two, hook up the old teardrop trailer Dad built Mom for a wedding present, and head up to Three Creeks Meadows or Takhlakh Lake for a three-day weekend. We'd usually arrive at night and climb right into our sleeping bags. The next morning, by the time it was light, I had to be up and figuring out where I was. I'd climb the highest tree or the closest hill to get my bearings. "Aha, that's where we are." I'd mentally check off the landscape: there's the mountain, there's the meadow, there's a little creek that goes down that way. Only after identifying north and south could I return to camp and settle down. I had to get the aerial view—I was in a tree as often as I was on the ground. Surely, I was supposed to have been a bird. Little wonder that I was flying Dad's airplane by age 17.

Once, when I was 10 years old, we were camped at cousin Erskine Wood's big pine meadow on the Metolius River in Central Oregon. Sitting on the bank, I noticed a beautiful yellow, black, and orange-headed bird in a pine tree across the river. I remember thinking, "Wow, that is really cool!"

Dad said, "That's a Western tanager."

From then on it was birds. My grandparents took me to Sauvie Island to see sandhill cranes. I did the Audubon Society Christmas bird count every year. Then, in seventh grade, an art teacher at Hillside School, Byron Gardner, noticed that I spent most of art class drawing birds. He didn't have any kids of his own and he, too, had a fascination with birds, so he took me out in his three-wheeled Pugeot to Eastern Oregon some weekends to look for falcons and hawks. Falconry is the most rarefied extension of an avian obsession.

When I was about 14, Byron sent me over my first cliff. We knew there was a prairie falcon eyrie a few miles east of Arlington, Oregon, and were determined to find it and bring our first young falcons home. We'd been searching all weekend, unsuccessfully, and Sunday afternoon—the sun was just starting to go down—we were still tramping on the cliffs above the Columbia River, trying to find the white droppings below a cavity that betray a nest site.

"Go up to that cliff and shoot the .22 rifle into the air," Byron said. "That'll usually get the bird off screaming if they're nesting there." We hiked to the cliff, shot the .22. Nothing. So we went up a little farther, shot the gun again, and sure enough, off came a male prairie falcon, kek-kek-kek-keking his high territorial call.

We got on top of the cliff, and could see five young nestlings just about the right age—about three weeks old.

"Well, you gonna climb down and get them?" I asked Byron.

"No way!" he said. "I'm scared just looking down that far! You

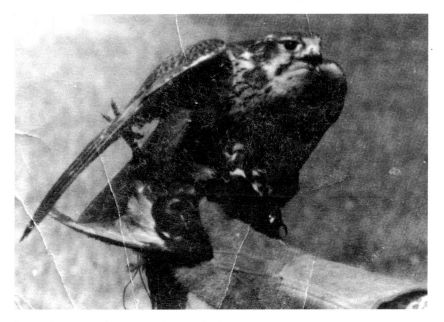

Baron, a tiercel prairie falcon, on the fist with a fresh pigeon kill.

need to do it. I'll tie a rope around your waist, we'll throw the thick one over the side and we'll just hand-over-hand you down." He handed me a basket in which to put two of the young falcons.

The female, or "falcon," prairie falcon, had now joined the male, or "tiercel," and they were diving at us at 70 mph, just 10 feet from our heads, carving parabolas in the desert air around the eyrie. Their cries came in an increasing crescendo. Okay, I thought, I guess I'm going over the cliff.

I tied a rope around my waist, slung the basket over my forearm, and grabbed the big rope and hung my terrified rear over the edge and tentatively climbed down to the ledge that nested the five downy, big-brown-eyed, startled fledglings. The sun was setting over the Columbia River. There were high cliffs and talus slopes across the river, rolling wheat fields in distant hills. I was scared, totally excited, feeling guilty and sorry for the adult falcons—eager but unsure of plucking two of their young from their rightful ancient home into a basket headed for a very different place.

We drove home with the young falcons, one male and the other female, and from then on it was full-time. Once you have responsibility for such a wild but dependent creature, it's all constant care and companionship. My little tiercel prairie falcon, Baron, was a handsome square-headed falcon, dark naral stripe down his face, both gentle and pugnacious with quick temper and agile flight. Baron was always keen to fly hard on the tail of whatever I could scare up, from pigeons to blackbirds, robins and ground squirrels. He taught me what he wanted to chase, how often he wanted to eat, and when he was secure enough to sleep. When he cocked his head and looked high in the sky, there was always a small dot, an eagle or hawk, circling high overhead. He sat on my gloved fist and preened, sneezed, shook his head, and scratched his cheek with a taloned foot. He roused his feathers and bobbed his head when trying to improve his focus on some indiscernible (to me) distant movement. I was a naive, impressionable youth, wide-eyed, and constantly in awe at the beauty and accuracy of the young falcon's every move.

Baron went everywhere with me. At first, he slept in my room, on a perch at the foot of my bed; later, Dad helped me build a hawk house in the yard. After school, we'd go to nearby fields to fly Baron. I would ready a padded leather lure with bits of fresh meat, hold him high on my fist, loose the swivel and leash, and off he would go, flying free but circling higher and higher, then stooping on the lure swung carefully past my body, just ahead of him as he feathered by, back and forth until he was tiring. And before he thought best to set out looking for something over a near horizon, I would slow the lure, let him take it and land on the ground to feast on a fresh morsel. Then I'd pick him up again carefully, slipping him more morsels from a leather bag at my waist. A slow-building relationship of mutual trust and understanding.

Instead of homework, I read bird books and made hoods, jesses, perches, silver bells, and other falconry accoutrements. Over the course of a year together, I watched Baron go through a molt, so I had every individual feather in a collection. I could pick up a falcon feather and tell you exactly what part of the body it came from, and whether it was from a prairie falcon or a peregrine.

Much of what I know today, I learned from birds.

Learning from Bananas

I graduated from college in 1968 with a degree in economics, was immediately classified 1A, and received a draft notice from the U.S. Army. Which meant I was headed to Vietnam. I'd tried to sign up for OCS—Officer Candidate School—to fly, but the closest I could get at the time without being a PhD from MIT was Army Photo Aerial Equipment Repair School in Fort Monmouth, New Jersey. It sounded like Camp Cannon Fodder to me.

But a few months earlier, I had, on a whim, applied to the Peace Corps. A friend and I were playing soccer, the spring of senior year and he said, "Hey, the Peace Corps recruiters are on campus."

"What's that about?" I said.

"Well," he replied, "better to be playing soccer with kids in Africa than shooting people in Vietnam."

I filled out the Peace Corps forms, hoping to build rope bridges in the mountains of Nepal or work with fishermen in the South Pacific, but then forgot all about it; I thought I was off to the jungle. Then the Peace Corps called and asked if I wanted to be an economist in the Central American Fisheries Program. I said, if I can go to the coast and actually fish with traditional fishermen, I'll do it. They agreed, and after a three-month training camp in Puerto Rico, I was sent to Sambo Creek, a small village on the Caribbean coast of Honduras.

My mission was to organize artisanal fishermen into cooperatives to help them get equipped to catch more and bigger fish and make more money. Sambo Creek was a Garifuna village, people of mainly African ethnicity who live along the Caribbean coast of Central America from Guatemala to Nicaragua. I helped introduce ice to preserve their catch for more distant markets, built bigger dugouts, and installed bigger engines, all in the name of progress. We got a loan from the Central American Fisheries Program to buy and hang a gill net to catch Spanish mackerel. It was challenging work, partly because there was so little money to buy the engines and sails and ice chests (not to mention the fact that the minister of fisheries stole most of the loan we'd gotten), but also because I was an introverted person. Speaking in public was frightening for me, let alone in a language I'd only begun to learn three months earlier. Yet public speaking was essential to the mission of organizing the fishermen, who actually didn't need much help from an inexperienced American kid to do something they'd been doing just fine for 300 years.

What, you might be asking by now, do fish have to do with bananas? For the first three months we were on site, the Peace Corps required us to perform an ethnographic study of our region—to figure out where the money was from and what the socioeconomic structure of the community was. I charted the age-class, gender diversity, jobs, family relationships, and sources of income of each of three Garifuna villages along the coast, across a distance gradient from the nearest larger town, La Ceiba. The primary source of cash for the region were jobs on the dock of the Standard Fruit Company, where dozens of Garifuna men were employed loading cardboard boxes full of bananas into huge freighters bound for Miami. I found that the closer a village was to the Standard Fruit dock, the worse shape the community was in. Farther away

Marta Arzu Buelto, with Juan, Nueva Armenia. Marta taught me much of what I know about poverty, race, and development.

from the dock, villages were well tended with traditional adobe homes in good repair, with fresh thatch on the roof and small gardens out back. There were plenty of fishermen, which, combined with the gardens, meant good nutrition. There were outhouses. The kids went to school. But near the wharf, where a higher percentage of men were employed, adobe homes were in poor repair

The author and Garifuna fishermen in Sambo Creek, Honduras, 1969.

and sewage ran in the streets. There were fewer farms and gardens, fewer artisanal fishermen. There was more drunkenness and a general deterioration of the traditional family structure—men took up with other women, abandoning their families. You'd see kids wandering around the streets on school days. It was almost a linear relationship between the health of the community and the distance from the docks. The modern cash economy was failing traditional Garifuna communities.

The economy of these villages turned out to be a lot more complex than it appeared. Not all the men fished, for example. Some of them were terrified of the ocean, so they worked as palm cutters for the thatched roofs, and were experts at it—where to find the right species and when to cut it. Others were carpenters, and they all had a complex system of barter with the fishermen. When the fishermen brought in their catch, it appeared that they arbitrarily passed out fish, with little money changing hands, but upon closer inspection, the fishermen had a careful accounting of services exchanged, or distribution based on familial structure. Additionally, to an uninformed observer like a Standard Fruit

Marta and José with family at home, Nueva Armenia. José was president of the fishing co-op we started. Marta looked after four generations of family in a 12' x 16' thatch-roofed, adobe house.

manager showing up as a tourist midday, it appeared that the men were idle, just lying in hammocks all afternoon. Because if you didn't live in the village, you never knew that the guy lying in the hammock at two in the afternoon was the same guy who got up at three in the morning, paddled through the surf in a small dugout canoe in the dark, sailed and paddled 10 to 15 miles off-shore to handline snapper and grouper, and returned before the catch rotted in the tropical sun.

So I took a closer look at the Standard Fruit dock workers. They spent all day long loading bananas that came on a train from interior Honduran plantations. They'd work for two weeks, and then they'd get paid. But very little of that money was actu-ally making it back to their families. Instead, flush with a wad of cash, they were squandering it with drinking and gambling. They might buy a fake gold watch, shiny black shoes, or blow it on booze and women, forgetting about the families depending on them back home. Which meant that their families couldn't pay the tab they'd been running up at the village grocery store for eggs, rice, beans, and flour. A possible solution occurred to me—instead of paying the men every two weeks, pay them weekly. It would be less tempting for them to blow the smaller sum, so more of the money might actually make it back to their families. The idea seemed simple. All I had to do was convince Standard Fruit.

The Standard Fruit offices were an oasis in the middle of La Ceiba—an all-white, royal-palmed American compound of schools, a social club, and pool. I went in and introduced myself to the senior manager—the top banana, so to speak—and explained that I worked in the villages and wanted to explore ways to improve their lot. He was a nice person, a congenial, middle-aged man from the South. He sat behind his desk in a white *guajabera* dress shirt and listened patiently.

But he quickly dismissed my suggestion and had no serious time or interest in the welfare of traditional village life. He said it would be quite impossible to change to a weekly pay schedule for a long list of bureaucratic non-reasons, the upshot of which was: you can't do something just because it's a good idea.

Cache: *Creating Natural Economies*

I walked back to the market where the mammy wagons—
Toyoto jeeps with huge wooden frames with benches for passengers and produce, chickens, bicycles, pigs, and small children on
the roof—gathered, and rode the dusty dirt road back to Sambo
Creek. It seemed like such a simple idea, at least worth trying,
with so much potential benefit to the welfare of hundreds of
women and families. The distance between healthy traditional
communities and the modern, asymmetrical economy weighed
infinite in that 15-mile, three-hour ride down a lonely tropical
road. It caused me to think that incremental, community- and
culture-based development that grew naturally from the bottom up, like bananas, might have more promise than reforming
the system from the power structure downward. Easy enough to
say; but power structures, I was to find, have ingenious ways of
perpetuating themselves. And hey, you can't do something just
because it's a good idea.

A small Garifuna dugout at the Sambo Creek fishermen's camp on Bolaño off the north coast of Honduras.

Learning as You Go

One day, about a year into Peace Corps, I got a letter from a friend named Phil Hoysradt with an ultimatum. Phil had bought plans for a Tahiti Ketch from *Popular Mechanics* for $10 and he was going to build it. If I wanted in, he'd need $500 right away. If I wasn't in, that was fine, he said, but he wasn't going to mess around.

I'd first met Phil in 1968 at Peace Corps training camp in Puerto Rico, both of us part of the 55 new trainees in the Peace Corps/United Nations Food and Agriculture Organization's Central American Fisheries Project. He was a serious fisherman from Gloucester, Massachusetts, and had sailed around the world on an oceanographic vessel. We kept in touch while I was posted in Honduras and he was stationed in Costa Rica and hatched an idea: after the Peace Corps, we'd use our readjustment allowance to buy a big dugout canoe, fix it up, and sail back up the coast to Oregon. So the ketch idea wasn't a total surprise and, given Phil's experience, seemed like a good bet. I sent him the money.

Over the next year, Phil got the hull roughed out with the help of master local carpenters. It was about one-third finished when, my stint with the Peace Corps over, I went down to join him. Janie Magavern, my girlfriend from college, came to Costa Rica shortly thereafter. She was no stranger to my harebrained schemes. Our first date had been a weekend trip to the Shawangunk Mountains, a famous rock-climbing spot near New Paltz, New York. Two friends, Teddy Ragsdale and Dave Rutherford—better known as "Rags" and "Rut"—and I were heading up there in my '63 red and cream Volkswagen bus. We had kayaks on the roof and Rut's great horned owl Archimeades inside. I called and explained the game plan to Janie and she said, sure, she'd go. Her response to the boat idea was pretty much the same. In short, Janie was game, and so now there were three of us working on the ketch.

Our shop was open-air, a small makeshift bench on the end of a dock on the estuary or "estero" side of the Puntarenas peninsula. We had one electric cord, a drill, hand planes, and saws.

Peregrin Took on our shakedown cruise off the northwest coast of Costa Rica.

We made the bolts out of brass stock that we'd tap and die. We used the lathe at the local sawmill—one that was sawing up huge, gorgeous, multicolored old-growth tropical hardwood logs rafted out of the coastal rainforest. We didn't really know what we were doing, but had a copy of *Boatbuilding* by Howard Chapelle. If we needed to mount an engine, we'd read that chapter, swing it into place, bolt it on, then realize, "Damn, that isn't right!" We'd re-read the chapter, pull the engine out, and put it in again. Then, take it out and do it a third time, by which time it generally worked. At one point, Phil flew home to Gloucester for the fishing season to make more money, and then it was just the Janie and myself.

They say you can get two of three basic things out of a sail-boat—speed, safety, and stability. We went for safety and stability. She was 30 feet long, 10 feet wide, and weighed 10 tons (including the old railroad tracks we scavenged for ballast). A ketch rig with two masts, a four-cylinder Volvo Penta diesel engine, 100-gallon fuel and water tanks, a tiny galley, and berths down below for four compatible companions. We decided to call her *Peregrin Took*, after Tolkien of course, but also because of the falcons. What helped me convince Phil was the meaning of the words; "to peregrinate" means to wander, so, *Peregrin Took* means, literally, "took a trip." Phil had to agree that it seemed like the perfect moniker.

Janie and I were married eight months later under a large pine tree at her family country house outside of Buffalo, New York. We had the perfect honeymoon getaway; in fact, we'd just built it. *Peregrin Took* was more or less completed a few days before Christmas, at least "finished" enough to feel confident with extra wood, paint, and supplies tied to the cabin roof; we wouldn't have to spend another Christmas in Puntarenas, and set sail for Cocos Island, then the Galapagos, and ultimately French Polynesia. It was in the Galapagos that I learned I had, miraculously, been accepted to the Yale Forest School, so Phil went back to fishing in Gloucester, to make some money, and catch up with us in Tahiti. Janie and I were on our own. We had all of three months' blue water sailing between us, and we'd spent almost two years helping to build her from bottom up with hand tools, and the toolbox was onboard. We shared a sense of confidence, a self-reliance that came slowly but surely from having done things ourselves, the hard way.

We spent a week hauled out on low tides on a beach in the Galapagos, painting the bottom and putting up stores of local food and water. Finally, on March 21, 1972, Janie and I set sail west to French Polynesia, an enamored pair of 26-year-old newlyweds on an extended do-it-yourself honeymoon.

On board for navigation was a sextant, a compass and a transistor radio. So on the last day in sight of land, it seemed like a good idea to take one more sun shot with the sextant, just to practice. I'd learned the technique a month before from Phil and had practiced it from Cocos to the Galapagos Islands. At this final moment, our precise location was known, between two of the westernmost islands of the Galapagos. But this would be the last time we'd see land for a month, so I suggested, "I'll do one more drill, just to make sure I've got it." Janie was steering under full sail with the hand tiller as a large pod of white-sided dolphins swam alongside. The tropical sun was setting on a clear Pacific horizon, light seas. I took the sightings and went below to make the calculations. Except that when I fixed our position on the chart, we weren't anywhere near the Galapagos. According to my calculations, we were somewhere off the southern coast of Chile, ostensibly 2,000 miles south of the islands that were, in fact, slipping past the portholes of the cabin.

It was a bit frustrating that I didn't have the hang of the celestial navigation yet, but figured we had thousands of miles to practice. We had a compass, and—as long as we were heading west, rather than north, east, or south—on an open ocean with no shipping lanes of consequence, we had room to learn, to adapt as we sailed. We'd adjust our course depending on winds and currents underway. That's when I went above deck as the sun sank in the west and flipped on the purple light on the big brass deck-mounted Plath compass, only to see the needle listing slightly to one side and bubbles percolating up from a leak in the seal.

"Janie," I said with determined calmness, "hand me that kerosene, the sealant, and a screw driver, would you?" Sitting in the wheel well with a flashlight in my mouth, I fixed the seal and filled it back up, screwed it back together, and we were headed west-southwest into the darkening sea.

We were anxious, but crazily confident. We had a back-up telltale compass in the galley, we were pretty sure the sun generally set in the west, and that the Marquesas were just three thousand miles, a few degrees south of west from the Galapagos. We knew we'd get it figured out. We'd built her from scratch, so should be able to fix most anything that broke. It was like learning to ride a bike; just pick up your feet and get rolling. You can't steer standing still. Move, try it out, learn as you go. Bertrand Russell once said, "It's not important if you are right or wrong, but critical that you are positive." He also said, "A life without adventure is likely to be unsatisfying, but a life in which adventure is allowed to take whatever form it will is sure to be short," but I was trying not to think about that one.

We were hit pretty hard about five days out in the Pacific in what was sometimes called "the all-American sleigh ride." There are generally fair southeasterlies in that latitude, but we encountered a week of 30- to 40-knot winds that built up huge breaking waves off the port bow. Sailors tend to exaggerate the height of waves, but we'd heel to starboard in the stiff winds, and plow up one side of a wave and then roller coaster down the other side. When we were down in the trough, the breaking white waves were as high as the mast, which was 30 feet. We took turns above and below deck, taking catnaps. Breaking waves drove drops of seawater through small joints in the planking next to

Janie at the helm in heavy weather on the Pacific passage.

our bunk. It was three or four hours on, three or four hours off with safety belts tied to lifelines. Janie was fearless.

We felt safer as the wind increased because it stiffened the boat and drove her constantly forward. *Peregrin Took* was heavy built, and although it was intimidating sitting there on the hand tiller licking rain and salt water from your face with waves washing down the deck, it gave us real confidence that the boat was holding together and actually firming up as conditions worsened. It was glorious at night just feeling the wind and watching the breaking waves and fluorescent wake, listening to the rush of water, watching the sky, and not worrying how fast we were moving. Just along for Mother Nature's ride.

Twenty-nine days later, on April 22, things were a lot calmer, the navigation fixes had become more consistent, and things were going swimmingly. Anticipation of land and a successful passage had us on our toes. "I think today we're going to see Ua Huka about 240 degrees and 30 miles off our port bow," I told Janie. Sure enough, that afternoon we started seeing boobies and frigates—coastal seabirds we hadn't seen since the Galapagos. The water's color changed a little, lightened, and about 2:30 or 3:00, Ua Huka was rising on the western horizon. *Ahoy Marquesas!* We brought out champagne we'd been saving for the occasion.

You could start to smell rich, moist soil, even 10 miles off shore. Not long after, we hooked into a big wahoo—maybe 40 pounds—on a long 300-pound monofilament line we were always trolling, and landed it onto the deck and pushed it flapping into the wheel well. Just about then the wind shifted and picked up. We tacked to the north without resetting a running backstay, one that we'd put in for safety but that wasn't part of the original sail plan. Janie couldn't get into the wheel well to steer because the wahoo was flailing wildly.

The wahoo that dismasted the *Peregrin Took* two hours before landfall on Ua Huka, Marquesas Islands.

"Hey," I shouted, "we better stop drinking champagne for a second and come up into the wind a bit more." Just then there was a sharp crack and the entire main mast sheared off four feet above the deck, sails and rigging crashing in the sea and banging against the hull. Dismasted on the final 20 miles of passage! We pulled the wreckage on deck, tied it all down, cranked up the diesel, and motored slowly to a gorgeous, small, protected bay surrounded by high, rolling, grassy hills and dropped the hook. Silence. Absolute calm at last.

Learning as we went. Indeed.

PART TWO

1991–2009

7

THE KITLOPE, ECOTRUST,
AND THE MAGIC CANOE

I left The Nature Conservancy not out of disagreement about the importance of preserving wild lands and threatened species or lack of admiration for its extraordinary accomplishments. I was and am a firm believer in both. What I came to realize, however, was that this approach pitted humans against nature—or at least humans who put nature first against humans who put development first. I could point to outcomes that benefitted both nature and human prosperity in any of the preceding stories: today the Sandy River system includes the protection of Portland's famous drinking water from the Bull Run Watershed, an important tributary of the Sandy; and on Sycan Marsh calf weight and pregnancy rates of mother cows may have increased for an estimated net gain to the ZX Ranch. But there's an element of revisionism in all this, since both my goal and that of The Nature Conservancy was not "reliable prosperity" as I've come to understand it, but simple land preservation; we both would have been happier if we could have gotten all those damn cows off of Sycan Marsh.

It was in Latin America that I began to be more aware of the inseparable connection between nature and human prosperity. I was also impressed by the importance of local buy-in and tapping local energy.

113

This wasn't a question of negotiating as I had with Nicolas Salgo. It was a question of understanding and respecting cultural differences. It demanded careful listening rather than fast talking. It required a trait that we Americans abroad are not famous for—humility.

I could have stayed with Conservation International and tried to put these principles more firmly into practice on the ground around the world, but for both personal and career reasons I was drawn back to my native Pacific Northwest and "the rain forests of home." Our mapping showed us that temperate rain forests around the world—in Chile, the South Island of New Zealand, Tasmania. and their former, extirpated extent in Norway, Greenland, and Western Ireland—were but one-thirtieth the area of tropical rain forests. North America had the largest temperate rain forest in the world, but half had been logged, roaded, dammed, or developed for agriculture. In the entire continental United States there was not a single pristine coastal temperate rain forest watershed of more than 10,000 acres in size. We'd burned the library of genetic information in our own rain forests. Brazil had 90 percent of their original Amazonian rain forests; we had about 10 percent. Why not work on our own rain forests and put a little humility into the American voice abroad?

I'd been thinking about these ideas for several years, but had not yet conceived the idea of starting my own organization. In one sense, Ecotrust was never conceived at all but, rather, hatched full-blown—like a phoenix—around a campfire in a magical place called The Kitlope.

Kitlope River, British Columbia

The floatplane pilot was eager to push off from the mouth of the Tsaytis River. The tide was falling fast and it was unknown territory for him. He'd dropped four of us off in this big, wild estuary strewn with huge logs, a fast blue-gray stream, and sandy beach covered with grizzly tracks and tormented willow. Coho salmon were running.

It was August 1990. The roar of the de Havilland nine-cylinder Beaver's radial engine echoed off high canyon walls as the float plane stepped up, the white wake grew smaller, the floats broke the tension of the water, throttle and prop backed off to

The Kitlope River estuary.

a quieter pace, we watched our only connection to civilization gradually vanish down channel.

Silence.

Then the sound of the stream running fast over granite boulders, underwater clinking of rocks, and scratching of glacial sand being carried to sea.

The four of us were all new to each other—three volunteers from the Western Canada Wilderness Committee and myself. We were there to get a look around the place. In surveying rainforests worldwide, Conservation International discovered that the Kitlope was the largest intact virgin rainforest watershed in the world. The bad news was that logging company West Fraser had a lease from the Canadian government to cut it all. In looking for local partners to help explore it, I'd enlisted the Western Canada Wilderness Committee, who had sent along my three companions as representatives. We were here to meet with a group of local leaders from the Haisla First Nation about mounting a grassroots campaign, but they couldn't meet us for three days, boating in from Kitamaat Village, 80 kilometers down the

The many changing channels of a naturally dynamic system: the Kitlope River.
It is the largest pristine coastal temperate rain forest in the world.

fjord. The four of us had decided to fly in anyhow and enjoy ourselves on a restful camping trip.

The volunteers consisted of two bewildered-looking young men, one brandishing a rusty German Luger to fend off the bears, and a brave young woman photographer from Vancouver. They'd said they would bring the food for five days' camping. All I could see was a cardboard box with a couple of loaves of bread, tuna fish, peanuts, and crackers. Looked marginal. At least I'd brought my own camping gear and fly rod.

I pitched a tent on a high bank under old-growth spruce six feet in diameter and 250 feet tall. Blueberries and salmon berries were abundant and ripe. In the low spots there was seven-foot-tall devil's club, with their painful thorns; best to steer clear of them. Bears had left trails winding along the high bank, but they should be little danger to us. My companions preferred the open sand bar near a willow patch that looked to them less like home to the bears.

About midnight of the first night I awoke to some frantic shouting and flashlights searching the sky. One of the threesome woke up to the gurgling of water and pointed a flashlight out the tent door in time to see one shoe and a cardboard box with our scarce supplies floating past on an outgoing tide. The next hour we spent carrying tents and sleeping bags and what food had survived through chest-deep water out of the 17-foot tidal zone to high-bank forest.

Coho were moving up the river and I was having a good time fly-fishing and bird-watching in the estuary and forests. But by the third day, our bedraggled crew was beginning to wonder if our alleged Haisla saviors were going to show up. At the appointed hour on a warm sunny afternoon, however, our first sign of human life appeared down channel. A small aluminum jet boat drove up the estuary, then up the mouth of the Kitlope River, with three Haisla Indians surveying their unlikely guests. John, the Luger-toting geologist, came running down the beach in his boxer shorts waving desperately. We later learned that Charlie Shaw, the jokester among the Haisla, had mischievously

A small aluminum Haisla fishing boat traveling the Gardner Canal into the Kitlope.

told the crew to "keep going," which they did just long enough for John to go nearly apoplectic.

Our "saviors" were Cecil Paul, a hereditary elder, Charlie Shaw, councilor, and Gerald Amos, elected chief of the Kitamaat Village Council of the Haisla First Nation. When we'd learned about the importance of the Kitlope, we'd asked around about what local people we could call. We'd been directed to the office of the Kitamaat Village Council, where Gerald was serving his second consecutive term as elected Chief Councilor. Just a week before I reached Gerald on the telephone, Cecil, who had been born in the Kitlope, walked into Gerald's office, his pockets stuffed with red ribbons.

Cecil had just returned from the Kitlope, his boat at full throttle all the way down the 80 kilometers of Gardner Canal that separated the Kitlope from Kitamaat Village, where the Haisla now lived. Cecil had found the ribbons lining the valley floor, marking out the road that West Fraser planned to build so they could log the ancient spruce and cedar that had been untouched for eons, except for bark taken for medicine, planks for houses, and the occasional canoe tree. "They're going to log our valley," Cecil said, "How are we going to stop them?"

Gerald looked back at him, "We'll just have to hope we can find somebody to help us," he said. A week later, I called the village office, asked for the chief, told them that our maps said they had the largest coastal temperate rain forest watershed in the world, and asked if someone might show us around.

So now, having arrived, they took us to a cabin next to the river under some big spruce where Cecil was born. Over the next few days we fished together and began to share stories around a campfire. I showed them the results of Conservation International's mapping study.

They set a small monofilament gillnet across a side channel. The water was glacial, milky gray-blue with visibility barely a few inches. The floats bobbed as coho and sockeye salmon entangled themselves and soon the floats were splashing across the entire reach. We would pull ourselves across the river with the net across the bow and pick fish. A hungry seal swam up from down river, poking his nose above the surface, sensing salmon in distress. I was watching, curious about what would happen next. *Booooom!*—a .222 magnum bullet shot past me and left the seal floating downstream and then, unfortunately for us, sinking as well, thus avoiding being eaten around the campfire as a side dish to fresh salmon. These salmon now belonged to Gerald and his family; brother seal would have to learn to let them alone.

By the time we were on the other side of the channel, the net behind us would again be full of bright six-to-ten-pound salmon. After a couple hours we had 100 to 125 chrome wild fish, 800-plus pounds of food for the smokehouse, for Haisla friends and families. They knew too well it was no longer this way in most of the salmon fisheries from Alaska to California. Cecil Paul described the Kitlope as their bank and their sanctuary, the secure place where they could go to find food, medicine, and peace of mind.

Around the campfire we talked about West Fraser Timber Company's tree farm license. This had been the Haisla's home for thousands of years, lands that had never been ceded, since, like most of western First Nations in Canada, the Haisla people had never signed a treaty giving up their rights of use and occupation. Nevertheless, the Kitlope was claimed by the British Crown and managed by the province's Ministry of Forests, like 80 percent of British Columbia. The entire Kitlope watershed was formally part of a 25-year "tree farm license" from the Crown to the timber company as part of a larger colonial social contract developed in the industrial era: you build the roads, the sawmills and pulp mills and the power stations, and employ the people, and the province gives you the land. That was the deal in Canada, much as it was in other colonies in the British Empire. West Fraser's tree farm license covered nearly four million acres, virtually the entire traditional territory of the Haisla people. After most of Cecil's Henaakisiala tribe of the Haisla people died during European-borne epidemics in the 1800s and early 1900s, the survivors were amalgamated with the Haisla on a 260-acre reserve, Kitamaat Village. West Fraser had logged much of the rest of the territory and were planning to log the Kitlope the following summer. Cecil showed us orange-painted sticks and marking tape scattered through the forest that marked the beginning of almost 300 kilometers of planned logging roads into virgin territory.

"Virgin territory" doesn't begin to say it. The Kitlope: 800,000 acres, a huge truly pristine watershed, the entire ecosystem from the glacial mountain headwaters to the sea. Magnificent old-growth cedar, hemlock, and spruce forests. At least four big, distinct tributary streams—the Tezwa running clear in the summer, including Kalitan Creek; the Tsatyis, with its confluence at the Kitlope's mouth and the extensive tidal flats and grasslands of the estuary; the Gamsby River, a big system near the headwaters flowing wild through U-shaped valleys and remote forests with another big run of coho; the Kapella River draining high lakes and bogs and a mysterious intermittent steaming, presumably hot springs, under deep glacial gravels near its confluence with the main-stem Kitlope 25 miles from the mouth. Resident seals on five-mile-long Kitlope Lake, river otter, mountain goat that leave their white winter fur in the lowland understory huckleberry bushes in winter, moose, all five species of native Pacific salmon—coho, sockeye, chum, humpies, and huge summer chinook—plus steelhead and trout. Yosemite-like granite cliffs going straight up two to three thousand feet, waterfalls, multicolored mountain ponds and cirques, vast snowfields and permanent glaciers, miles and miles of alpine tundra vegetation, crowberry, Japanese-garden-like contorted low trees, ptarmigan (a mountain grouse), and nesting peregrine falcon above tree line. Black bears, grizzly, cougars, an occasional rare mountain caribou from the interior, giant caves, bogs with insect-trapping pitcher plants, black merlin (a small rare falcon nesting beside the bogs in old crow and raven nests, hawking dragon flies in the summer). White sand beaches on the lake, and "stone-man"—a rock figure high on a ridge above the lake said by Haisla elders to a be a wayward hunter who disobeyed the *nuyem*, the stories and laws of the time, and turned to stone.

What had led us to a place as remote as the Kitlope in the first place had been a mapping analysis of the character, distribution, and status of temperate rain forests worldwide. It had to be worldwide, a view of the entire extent of this forest type. Otherwise, we would never know the particular importance of one example of the forest or another—e.g., largest example of its kind in Tasmania, in the southern hemisphere, or the world? In 1990, we published the results of this study, an atlas, the first of its kind for temperate rain forests.

Having completed the assessment, we set about mapping and describing in more detail the distribution and status of what we called the "rain forests of home." We also mapped declining salmon runs and the pattern of loss of the 63 distinct languages spoken by coastal people associated with salmon and these forests. We published maps showing that the pattern of loss of language, salmon, and forests was similar: increasing degrees of endangerment from north to south across all measures. Vast swaths of temperate rain forest in southeast Alaska on the Tongass National Forest, the largest public forest in the United

States, had been devastated by clear cutting for timber and pulp, mostly by Japanese companies that had been given subsidized public timber as part of post–World War II reconstruction. U.S. taxpayers had been effectively paying companies to cut the magnificent rain forests of Alaska. In 1991, the best remaining rain forest watersheds were in northern British Columbia.

With the atlas in hand, we then contracted with a young Canadian forester to map every coastal temperate rain forest watershed over 12,000 acres in size, using satellite imagery, Ministry of Forests data, and interviews with scientists and environmentalists. We broke watersheds into size and degrees of disturbance. This resulted in a publication we shared widely with Canadian government agencies, the conservation community, First Nations leaders, and scientists. It showed that of the 354 coastal rain forest watersheds in British Columbia, just 85 remained intact, and of the 25 watersheds over 250,000 acres in size, just one remained intact: the Kitlope River on the central inland coast.

This was news to everyone. Virtually no one had heard of the Kitlope. The environmental community was focused on one small old-growth watershed on the west coast of Vancouver Island, the Carmanah Valley. It had magnificent large trees but was on an island, insular, therefore less rich biologically than the continental mainland Kitlope. The minister of forests was perplexed. He said he had been trying to get the ministry to do an analysis like ours for years at great expense. It took CI six months and $40,000, hard work for a single author, but the "whole ecosystem" lens of watershed, an entire river basin, had created for us an image that was clear, definable, searchable, and represented a viable biological unit on a global scale.

Our Haisla companions assured us they, too, did not want to see the Kitlope logged. But their bigger problem was teenage suicide, alcohol, and drugs. Seven children had taken their lives in their small community of 750 residents in the past few years, and they wondered aloud if there would be a Haisla culture another generation hence. Ninety percent of their proud people had died

"Yosemite of the North" is what some call the passageway to the Kitlope River, British Columbia.

within a century of contact with the first white settlers; by the mid-1920s, Gerald's grandmother had been one of a handful of unmarried, childbearing Haisla women to survive.

Cecil Paul looked up from the campfire and toward the small cabin built on the site where he was born. When he was ten, he told us, the Royal Mounted Police came to Miskusa, the small village at the mouth of the Kitlope River, and rounded up all the 10-year-old Indian boys and took them to residential school in Port Alberni on Vancouver Island. Cecil, who had no shoes and spoke only his own Henaakisiala dialect of the Haisla language, was torn from his family and sent to a strange place 500 miles away—all part of the assimilation policy of the time to break the Indians of their primitive ways and make them into proper citizens of Canada.

The other boys in Port Alberni spoke no Haisla; they were from many different villages up and down the coast. They were required to learn English and were forbidden to speak their native language. One day Cecil ran into another boy who spoke Haisla and he quietly asked him what was going on. A priest spotted them, took the two boys to the center of a large room, told the other boys to make a big circle, took the two young Haislas' pants down and beat them. These were the same residential schools whose sex abuse scandals Canadian Prime Minister Steven Harper apologized for more than a century later in 2008. Cecil grew to despise white men. Later, he took to the bottle and lived on the East Vancouver streets for almost 20 years.

I suppose you had to be there to understand the full effect of these stories. All I know is that as I listened to Gerald, Cecil, and Charlie describe their own·circumstances, it came to me as if it were the most obvious thing in the world: working with Conservation International wasn't going to cut it. In order to have the organizational capacity to meet the full range of support that the Haisla needed to address their social, economic, and environmental needs, I was going to have to start a new organization focused on both the people and the rain forests of North America. I proposed the idea, and Gerald and I made a deal: if he would serve on my board and help me build yet another new organization, I would do what we could to help him address the social needs of the Haisla and protect the Kitlope from logging.

I founded Ecotrust in 1991, the same year that I resigned from Conservation International, with Gerald as one of the original board members. We organized a multidisciplinary three-day conference at Whistler, British Columbia, in September of 1992. There were First Nations leaders, government scientists and resource managers, oceanographers, paleontologists, salmon geneticists, economists, and anthropologists—in short, everyone under the sun (or the coastal clouds) with some relevant expertise about the social, ecological, and economics of the bioregion. The result was a book called *The Rain Forest of Home*, published in hardback, then republished in paperback, by Island Press. All of this research, data gathering, and synthesis was an effort to frame the issues and ideas about temperate rain forests. It led, quite unexpectedly, to a very clear picture of the global and urgent importance of the Kitlope and leaders of the Haisla First Nation.

Next, Ken Margolis, my old colleague and our lead staff person in British Columbia, and I helped create a strategy based on the assumption that the Haisla were the true owners of the Kitlope, and that they would demonstrate responsible ownership. They started by working on a scientific and cultural reconnaissance of the watershed, bringing leading Canadian scientists up to look at the forests, the wildlife, the fish, and the insects. At the same time elders were interviewed to supply the traditional place names that had been used for countless generations. Important spawning areas were mapped for the first time, along with traditional place names. The area was characterized in a handsome but inexpensive publication that by its very existence asserted the reality of Haisla territorial rights of use and occupancy and was also useful in interesting others in this little-known ecosystem.

While West Fraser and the ministry began to examine it, we were busy pulling together a detailed report describing the potential management scenarios for the Kitlope and sponsoring discussion groups and consensus-building efforts in Kitamaat Village and nearby towns. We flew elders around their territory so they could see the logging that was taking place just over the border of the Kitlope watershed and know what they were up against.

In the meantime we were courting *Time* magazine reporters and Canadian press and conducting a number of trips with the Haisla into the Kitlope, including a trip with John Cashore, the minister of environment and later minister of aboriginal affairs. Hank Ketchum, the chair of West Fraser, was always both thoughtful and cordial, and we worked down the line to try to tactfully bring his foresters and mill managers along to the thought that they would never log the Kitlope. Cecil Paul was more direct: on one trip to Victoria to see the minister of forests, he informed the minister he would be on the beach with his gun if they ever entered to log the Kitlope.

We also decided that, as owners, the Haisla should hold a public hearing. We called Senator Jim Fulton, a friend of First Nations, and he agreed to attend. Then we called the mayor of Kitamat—the nearby city—and told him Senator Fulton was

A critical moment in negotiations to protect the Kitlope—Gerald Amos, chief; John Cashore, British Columbia's minister of the environment; author; and Cecil Paul, Haisla elder, on the shore of Kitlope Lake, 1993.

coming. He agreed to show up. So we built the invitations, and by the day of the hearing everybody who mattered was crowded into the chamber we rented in Kitamaat.

The representatives of West Fraser spoke first. They said simply that they needed to keep their mills running and their employees at work. Various public officials spoke and they too had something to add. Then it was the turn of the Haisla Nation.

Louisa Smith, Cecil Paul's sister, rose. She spoke of her upbringing in the Kitlope, of its importance as a last repository of all the elements of traditional subsistence. She spoke of her mother's grave and of the deep spiritual power of the Kitlope, where she and other members of the Haisla Nation resorted as often as they could to restore their own spirits and to commune with those of their ancestors.

As Louisa spoke, something strange began to happen. There were perhaps 35 people crowded into the room, and as she told her stories, many of them started to cry. The room was very quiet except for Louise's soft voice.

Among those with tears running down their faces was a huge, tousled logger named Bruce Hill. After the meeting, Bruce came up to Gerald and Ken. "I never understood before," he said. "I want to do whatever I can for you."

Gerald had already decided that we needed a nonprofit organization working in and beyond Kitamaat Village to protect indigenous territory, help young people rediscover their culture, and work for kinds of economic development that would provide jobs without eating up the natural resources. He even had a name picked out; in the Haisla language, *na na kila* means "watchman," and the new organization was to become the Na na kila Institute. Within a few weeks, Bruce Hill had put down his chainsaw and become the first executive director.

Other initiatives were going on simultaneously. To address the concern about the next generation of Haisla leaders, we helped create the Haisla Women's Society for Rediscovery, and brought Rediscovery camps to Kitlope Lake—programs that ran for seven years, helped reduce teenage suicides, and brought a new sense of pride and identity to Haisla youth.

As for our negotiations with Cashore and West Fraser, there were many doubters among the Haisla themselves, people with deep and understandable distrust of outsiders, of whites, of environmentalists. There were those who would be happy to log the Kitlope if it brought a few jobs and a little additional income to an impoverished community. But a major turning point came at the public meeting when West Fraser ultimately offered a compromise: they would log only 50 percent of the Kitlope and hire all native workers.

The representative stood and walked up to the front of the auditorium. "We've got to have that Kitlope wood," he said. "We need it to keep our mills running. I'll tell you what we're going to do: every job in the Kitlope will go to a Haisla. You'll build the roads, you'll drive the trucks, you'll take the logs out. It will give your community full employment for the next 20 years."

Unemployment had hovered around 40 percent for years; people were desperate for jobs. The hall was silent and it looked like with this one bold move, West Fraser had put the effort to protect the Kitlope in check.

Gerald Amos, former chief councilor of the Haisla First Nation and founding Ecotrust board member.

Then a young Haisla woman stood up and said, "We don't want your jobs! We just want you to go away and leave us alone!" She sat and Morris Amos, Gerald's brother stood up and reiterated what she had said. For the next 40 minutes one Haisla person after another stood up and said that they didn't want the jobs, they wanted the Kitlope.

There were two telephone booths in the building, and two Haisla elders occupied them during the lunch break. When the meeting reassembled, they went up to the front of the room. "We called over 40 Haisla families," they said. "Nobody wants your jobs. We want the Kitlope protected." The offer was turned down flat.

At last, on August 16, 1994, after four years of continuous work by Haisla leadership and Ecotrust staff and board, there was a big announcement. B.C. Premier Michael Harcourt proclaimed that the Kitlope would be protected forever. The province would sign a nation-to-nation co-management agreement with the Haisla, and Hank Ketchum and the West Fraser Timber Company generously announced they would *voluntarily and without compensation* give up their right to log the Kitlope Valley. It had little to do with the Haisla campaign, they explained. Their own internal review of our mapping had shown that there was one coastal temperate rain forest watershed the size of the Kitlope in the world, and it was better to leave it alone.

The province called the agreement the Kitlope Heritage Conservancy. Ken Margolis and I had spent many long, late evenings with the Kitamaat Village Council over weak coffee and stale donuts trying to learn what the Haisla wanted to name their new Heritage Conservancy. After months of meetings and discussion, Gerald announced their decision. The Haisla would call it *Hu'sduwachsdu Nuyem Jees*.

"What is that?" I asked Gerald and Cecil.

"It is what we have always called this place," he said. "*Hu'sduwachsdu* means Land of Milky Blue Waters and *nuyeem jees* are the sacred stories that go with that place. The stories tell us what it takes to survive and live well in this particular part of our territory," he said. "They have accumulated and been handed down for thousands of years; that is our *nuyem*. That is what we call it and we see no reason to change now. The Kitlope hasn't changed. It is just you white guys who have done something on paper, and if it makes you feel better to put a name on it, that's fine."

Hu'sduwachsdu Nuyem Jees, land of milky blue waters and the stories that go with that place.

For this white guy it was more than fine. The Kitlope is an entire, healthy, functioning ecosystem. It is a landscape-scale connector between the fire-adapted interior lodge-pole pine forests of huge Tweedsmuir Provincial Park in the B.C. interior and the coastal rain forests of the outer coast in Fjordlands Provincial Park: a protected wildlife corridor 100 miles east and west from the Pacific Ocean to the dry interior. It is a place still dominated by natural ecological processes, heavy snow, torrential Pacific rain, huge rock avalanches in the spring melt that clear wide swaths of forests, constantly changing stream courses, giant old-growth spruce along the banks undercut by spring floods cartwheeling down the river bank to bank, a giant limbed thrashing machine clearing fresh gravel for spawning salmon. It is an extraordinarily dynamic system of destruction and renewal, a patchy, diverse landscape at once serene and peaceful and at other times wild, dangerous, and formidable. The Kitlope is the largest undisturbed coastal temperate rain forest watershed in the world: the only remaining example more than 250,000 acres in size in North America that has not been logged. No roads, dams, permanent structures of any kind, other than the watchman cabin we helped build.

Yet visiting the Kitlope without the Haisla people is a fragment of the experience one has when accompanied by Gerald or Cecil Paul or any of the Haisla leaders. Without the stories of 10,000 years of occupation, the Kitlope is an empty, lonely place, another giant swath of wilderness. In the first months of work, the Haisla produced the Kitlope Declaration to state their community-wide support for preventing logging. It said, "We do not own the land; the land owns us." They believe they are part of a larger community of life. They believe in managing their natural relations, not their natural resources.

Four years, 800,000 acres, $600,000—the amount Ecotrust put into our campaign—adds up to 75 cents an acre. It was an impressive achievement by any standard. However, not all of our ventures in the Kitlope were unmitigated successes. During the peak of the Rediscovery camps on Kitlope Lake, Ken Margolis and I were sitting on the beach with some of the Haisla kids

Sockeye salmon entering Kalitan Creek, a small tributary of the Tezwa River, in the Kitlope watershed.

watching campers paddle across the lake in one of the fiberglass Old Town canoes we'd bought for the camp. We talked about how great it would be for them to have a traditional carved and painted cedar canoe and paddles at the camp instead of these new high-tech versions. Ken ran with that idea, invited West Fraser to donate a valuable old-growth cedar log, and asked around the village if there was a carver who might want to build the canoe. He found one and signed a contract to carve it.

And, sure enough, two years later a beautiful painted canoe was launched with great ceremony in the village. Ken watched as it ceremoniously tipped over and almost sank. The elders were unanimous in their disapproval: "That canoe is evil. Don't let the children go in that canoe—take it away!" Margolis, crestfallen, asked them what had gone wrong. "That carver was an artist not a canoe maker," the elders replied. "We could have told you that." No matter how hard we tried to listen and respond to the true needs of the community, there was always a deeper level of understanding we can perhaps never achieve.

I reminded Gerald Amos of the canoe incident when my son Sam and I visited him in August of 2008. Gerald thought about it as he listened to the ravens calling from the trees and watched the evening light over the ocean. Then he said, "We might have made mistakes and, yes, there were problems. But it is really about relationships. When people come to a pole repatriation ceremony as our guests, they have privileges, they have special rights, but they also have responsibilities. They come as witnesses. When we need them, or they need us, we expect them to be there. We will be there for them. In the end, the relationships that we build are all we have."

The magic canoe that wasn't. Kitamaat Village, British Columbia.

Though it's taken me a long time to learn this, I've come to see that Gerald is right: culture is more powerful than data, science, money, and technology. Indeed, culture shapes all these things, and the landscape as well. It is our interdependence and the character of our relationships with each other and our environment that matter. I call this "reliable prosperity."

Cecil Paul calls it the "magic canoe." He says the Haisla were alone in their struggles for recognition and assistance in protecting their "bank," their source of subsistence food, medicine, and spiritual renewal—the Kitlope. Then some strange white people appeared out of nowhere and stretched out a hand—"Boston people," because the first whites the Haisla met were from Boston. Then more strangers came: scientists, and foundation people, and museum directors, and Sami people from Sweden, and filmmakers, and television people, and reporters, and government ministers. Cecil says they were building a magic canoe, and the more people that came, the bigger it got. And he asked Gerald Amos to steer the canoe and be his people's spokesman on everything to do with the Kitlope. "When the Kitlope was saved we put the canoe ashore," says Cecil. "But it will be ready when we wish to go on a journey together another day."

Haisla youth at the mouth of the Kitlope River.

8

WILLAPA BAY:
The Resource Curse and a Hopeful Example Abroad

The perceptive reader—perhaps even the unperceptive reader—will notice that the centerpiece of Ecotrust's work with the Haisla was land preservation: the Kitlope Heritage Conservancy. But it was land preservation with a difference: instead of launching a traditional save-the-rain-forest environmental campaign from the top down, we adopted the strategy of supporting the Haisla people to see if we could help them gain protection in an entirely new way—by helping the local residents, indeed 10,000- to 15,000-year indigenous residents, address their needs and the resiliency of their own community, whatever that might be. This was a new approach, one that engaged the forces of social and economic development not on the footing of enemies in attack or retreat, but of allies who, like the Haisla themselves, recognize humanity as an inseparable part of the natural world. I say "new," but in fact the principle had been articulated some 40 years earlier by the pioneer environmentalist Aldo Leopold when he urged a change in "the role of Homo Sapiens from conqueror of the land-community to plain member and citizen of it."

These were the principles that guided and informed the founding of Ecotrust. The new organization's strategic vision piece, New Bearings, *reflects this: "Ecotrust is founded on the belief that local communities can and must build the capacity to meet the economic and social needs of the people who live there while replenishing the natural resources on which the future of the community depends." Or again: "Local people don't want to save the environment any more than they want to conquer it; what they want to do is live in it."*

The Kitlope, then, became a whole new kind of protected area that recognizes the rights and responsibilities of the people who have occupied the place for millennia, a nation-to-nation co-management agreement in which the provincial, federal, and First Nations governments share responsibilities.

But most modern communities are a far cry from indigenous people who for millennia may have lived in quasi equilibrium, a reciprocal relationship with their environment. How could we apply the lessons we learned from the Kitlope and the Haisla to modern market conditions— specifically, to rural communities whose economies are based on natural resources and whose markets may be national and even global in reach? I wanted to find a community in which to test these principles, a place where we could demonstrate, at least on a small scale, that the long-term goal of reliable prosperity is inevitably bound up with the goal of conservation and the restoration of ecosystems.

I found such a place close to home, right across that great river, the Columbia, which divides Oregon and Washington.

Willapa Bay, Washington

In the fall of 1852, a man named James Swan arrived at Willapa Bay, then known as Shoalwater Bay, in the brig *Oriental*. He built a cabin at the mouth of the Bone River, and became one of the first permanent white settlers. He kept a diary, later published as *The Northwest Coast*, in which he marveled at the area's extraordinary natural abundance: "The shoals are covered with shell-fish . . . several varieties of clams, crabs of the largest size . . . shrimps, mussels, and a small species of sand-lobster . . . in the greatest abundance. Salmon of several varieties abound. . . . Sturgeon of a very superior quality are plenty."

The author and Tundra, an immature peregrine falcon trapped at Leadbetter Point, Willapa Bay, 1963.

Today Willapa Bay is the cleanest large estuary in the lower 48 states, one of the five biggest oyster producers in the world, surrounding lands a source of deep red cranberries particularly well-suited to Ocean Spray's juice, and original home to Weyerhaeuser's largest tree farm. This was the place where Frederick Weyerhaeuser got off the train from his home in St. Paul, Minnesota, took one look around at the forest of huge Sitka spruce, red cedar, western hemlock, and Douglas fir, and said, "I will buy it!" And did, for a purported 50 cents an acre. The Long Beach Peninsula separates Willapa from the Pacific Ocean, the longest beach on the Washington coast. Oysterville was established on the tip of the peninsula to supply the newly rich San Francisco miners during the California gold rush with fresh oysters. According to local legend, in the late 1800s there were more inhabitants on the Long Beach Peninsula than in Portland or Seattle.

Thirty years after James Swan settled in Willapa Bay, my great grandfather Charles Francis Beebe was sent by his father from New York to Portland to establish Sutton & Beebe, later The Beebe Company. The big store was in Astoria, Oregon, at the mouth of the Columbia River just south of Willapa. Both Dad and Grandpa Beebe worked at the Beebe Company, which prospered in the early years because of the extraordinary salmon fishery in the Columbia, off coastal Oregon and Washington, and Willapa Bay.

Willapa has special meaning for me not only because of the family history there, but also because it was here that I first trapped a wild peregrine falcon in the fall of 1963. Tundra was a female or "falcon," probably born on a high cliff on an interior Alaska river and was on her first southerly migration—a "passage" bird in falconry terms—at just four months old. She was the last of almost 30 hawks, owls, eagles, and falcons that had trained me in the art and practice of falconry from age 13 until college in 1964. I trapped her with a well-noosed pigeon one clear Sunday in late September on the northern tip of the Long Beach Peninsula, Leadbetter Point, where Willapa feeds into the Pacific. After years of searching the Oregon and Washington coast for peregrine, this was the best habitat I had ever seen for migrating waterfowl and shorebirds that the falcons would follow south.

A quarter century later, in 1989, as I was beginning to explore

Leadbetter Point and the mouth of Willapa Bay.

137

places in the coastal temperate rain forests of North America where we could prove up the case for conservation-based development, I thought surely Willapa Bay was a place to focus our efforts. If we couldn't see it come true here, a 680,000-acre watershed with just 20,000 residents, I thought perhaps it couldn't be done anywhere. Dairy and cattle farms, oysters, cranberries, fish, forests, and tourism—this was a place where empowering local residents with access to information, technology, and capital, the very forces driving globalization worldwide, would surely become a wonderful example for the growing movement of "sustainable development."

From 1991 until about 1996, as Ecotrust was itself getting established in a small office on Portland's waterfront, our growing staff of eight to twelve helped create a number of initiatives with local residents of Willapa Bay that were strategic ways to support an integrated, community-based process of conservation and economic development.

Our dreams were boundless. We would help build the capacity of local residents to protect the small fragments of remaining old-growth forests and diminishing wild salmon runs while supporting selective logging, value-added fish and shellfish processing, and ecotourism. It was a collaborative effort between Ecotrust and some of my old colleagues at The Nature Conservancy. We carefully divided up our respective commitments: together we would support the development of a community-based, nonprofit organization—what became the Willapa Alliance. The Conservancy would take the lead on land conservation, while Ecotrust would pursue strategies to support local businesses. We would address the needs of native people and poor and moderate-income residents. We would help oystermen protect the estuary's water quality, and reduce the threats of invasive tidewater grasses, keep the shorelines undeveloped, and reduce wastewater and contaminated runoff from farms and development, while helping cranberry growers produce organic cranberries. We spent years helping a local school develop a 1,000-year plan for restoring Chinook salmon to the Chinook River in nearby

Bone River, Willapa Bay, now a Nature Conservancy preserve.

Chinook, Washington, home to the Chinook Indian tribe—what we called "Chinook to the fourth power."

The Conservancy completed important acquisitions of ecologically sensitive lands in the Bone River, Niawakum River, and Ellsworth Creek basins. We gave fellowships to two smart young people from back East, one around eco-development, the other on policy issues. We helped them develop a huge database of ecological and socioeconomic conditions, acquire computer hardware and GIS software, and train local staff to produce magnificent four-color, watershed-scale maps showing land ownership, trends of employment, and sectoral patterns of forests, fish, farms, and tourism. It all came together in a handsome little book called *The Tidewater Place*, the principle criticism of which was that the photos made even clear-cuts look good. We raised millions of dollars, and Vice-President Al Gore's White House Council on Sustainable Development made Willapa their first field trip. The Willapa Alliance grew to eight or ten local staff with a diverse board representing local leaders from oystering to logging, hotels, cranberry

139

growers, cattlemen, and retail shop owners. Paul Newman and his daughter Nell flew down to visit in Danny Vollum's 1936 twin-turbine Grumman Goose vintage airplane for a surprise visit. Paul had a big oyster lunch with Alliance members and enjoyed walking the oyster flats, taking in the birdlife, and meeting local business people. Willapa residents were thrilled.

Officers of major foundations traveled across the country to take it all in. On a cold winter day with the rain blowing sideways, we dragged poor Walt Coward, a senior officer from the Ford Foundation in New York, two hours up a dirt logging road where we described our efforts to triple available salmon spawning habitat by improving culverts, which often block the fish's upstream progress. Walt looked into the sky and said, "So this is what these global dreams come to? The muddy, backbreaking work of putting new culverts under dirt logging roads 40 miles from sea?"

Peter Drucker once said that all great visions deteriorate ultimately to daily drudgery. Willapa was ours. And it didn't all work. What I didn't understand despite my major in economics at college was what economists call the "resource curse": such

Norris "Mugs" Petit, Willapa Bay fisherman and early board member of the Willapa Alliance.

abundance of natural resources—be it fish, trees, diamonds or oil—that people get rich by getting more at the expense of getting better. It is the similar challenge that plagues what Thomas Friedman, in his book *Flat, Hot and Crowded*, calls "petro-dictators" in the Middle East, Nigeria, and Russia. "As the price of oil goes up, democracy goes down," says Friedman. Quick natural resource wealth, no need for taxes, no need for representation; it creates competition but little cooperation. The abundant natural resources of Willapa Bay that I thought would be a powerful force of community self-interest were actually the source of a deeply divided community.

The Willapa Alliance ultimately deteriorated into traditional conflicts between oystermen trying to keep the bay's water clean and real estate developers. Deep suspicion and paranoia about local versus outside interests were rampant; disputes about who got the money, sectoral self-interest versus "community" self-interest, our inability to attract sufficient staff leadership, and the ephemeral attention span of donors all conspired to compromise the grand vision. To local working folk, Conservancy staff came off as aloof, urban, elite preservationists. Perhaps I did as well. I tired of the constant infighting, competition for control, ingratitude, and bickering.

Some of the foundations began supporting the Alliance directly rather than through Ecotrust, so we lost influence on budgets, hiring, and strategic direction. Board members of the Alliance were representing their "stakeholder" interests rather than the broader mission of the organization. One of Ecotrust's founding board members, a prominent Willapa oysterman and board member of the Alliance, was voted off the chairmanship when he tried to push priorities excessively his way. One of his favorite stories was working summers through college to earn enough money to buy an elderly neighbor's waterfront acreage because his father refused to loan him the money. A year later, with money finally in hand, he went to the old woman only to find out the land had been sold to his father. "Never tell anyone about a real estate deal!" admonished his dad. His membership on Ecotrust's board was not renewed. I needed people

who served Ecotrust's and the Alliance's interest, not their own—
contrary to the real estate lessons of their fathers.

We helped local residents appreciate what a special place their
home was on a national, even a global basis. We helped Mugs Petit,
a one-eighth Chinook Indian, commercial crabber, fisherman,
and Willapa Alliance board member, connect with New Seasons
Markets in Portland, where he got $3 per pound for fresh wild
Chinook salmon, instead of the dock price of $.80 per pound.
And he is still selling to New Seasons almost 20 years later. "The
Alliance was not a failure," says Mugs. "It was a wake-up call."

The Alliance saved some important fragments of Willapa's
former glory, and we built some lasting relationships. But our
original thought that "if it can't be done here, it can't be done
anywhere" was exactly wrong. For as long as the residents believe
that short-term wealth will come again from logging big trees at
a rate faster than they grow and fishing at harvest levels higher
than the fish can possibly reproduce, as long as they expect
technology to successfully replace nature, reliable prosperity
will come slowly, if at all, to Willapa Bay. Unlike the Kitlope,
where the Haisla brought a deep, shared cultural context that
made consensus building and common cause a source of local
energy, the social and cultural history of Willapa, a case study in
the resource curse, made releasing the energies of local people
toward common cause more difficult than anticipated.

Willapa haunts me even today. It seemed to be all there, the
prospect of reliable prosperity from evolving attitudes and culture that connects people's fates as the residents come to more
fully appreciate what a healthier, more diverse, functioning, whole
natural Willapa ecosystem might look like. My dream of a natural
model of forestry, fishing, farming, and tourism driven by a bottom-up process of social engagement was only partly embraced
in Willapa. Consequently, I took some consolation in discovering
that what I'd been attempting in Willapa could actually be done,
though it is being done in a very different place under different
circumstances, and it turns out it takes more money, brains, and
persistence than I have been able to muster so far.

Land, Lots of Land

In January 2009, my son Sam and I were waiting around in Puerto Varas, a picturesque old German port town in central Chile. We were there to revisit Parque Pumalín, the nearly million-acre preserve single-handedly assembled by Doug Tompkins, former owner of outdoor equipment and clothing purveyors, the North Face, and then later, Esprit. Doug, however, was delayed on his return from the Antarctic sea, where he had been harassing Japanese whalers with Paul Watson and the Sea Shepherd Conservation Society. They trailed the whalers everywhere, tossing stink bombs on the deck and filming the chase. He was delayed just enough to give Sam, me, and our colleague Ian Gill time to watch President Obama's inauguration on television. At that moment, it felt like a great time to be American.

Ohioan by birth, via upstate New York and then California, Tompkins is a world-class mountain climber, outdoorsman, designer, pilot, photographer, author, entrepreneur, and environmentalist

Parque Pumalín, almost one million acres of temperate rain forest, mountains, and lakes that Doug Tompkins has acquired from private landowners and is donating to the Chilean people as a new national park.

143

who describes his devotion to the planet and its creatures as a "religious position." Tompkins built North Face, and then sold it in 1972. Then, with his first wife, Susie Tompkins, he built clothing retailer Esprit with worldwide stores and annual sales in excess of $1 billion. In 1992, shortly after his divorce from Susie, he sold his interest in Esprit for a reported $175 million, moved to Chile and set about changing the world.

I first met Doug in the Kitlope River in 1991. Encouraged perhaps by Ecotrust's mapping of the large pristine rain forest watersheds in North America and the identification of the Kitlope as the largest of its kind left in the world, Doug had flown his own float plane to British Columbia to get a firsthand look. Over dinner he wished me luck preserving the Kitlope, our work with the Haisla First Nation, logging concessionaires, and the Provincial government. Doug said he was going to Chile where land was cheap, title was legally secure, and he could use his own money and force of will to do what was necessary to preserve large swaths of the Chilean temperate rain forests, the second-largest area of this relatively rare and endangered forest type after North America's coastal forests.

Chile was not new to Tompkins; it was country he knew and loved. There were Andean peaks he and his friend Yvon Chouinard had climbed since the 1960s, mountains they had named, rivers they had pioneered in kayaks, and streams they had fished long before most North Americans had heard the word "Patagonia." Yvon, of course, made that word commonplace around the world with the growing success of the outdoor clothing company named after the place he and Doug had come to know as their own.

Doug set about identifying and buying large tracts of ecologically important rain forests in southern Chile. By about the time the Kitlope was protected, he had assembled a magnificent area of similar size to the Kitlope, some 50 miles north and south, from estuaries, river valleys, to high mountain lakes, waterfalls, and permanent glaciers. On the valley floors, where rivers meet the long fjords of Chile's rugged coast, he bought old farms—holdings in the larger surrounding landscape.

144

For the first decade, Doug's intention to create large areas of parklands in Chile and later in Argentina was the subject of some national suspicion. At times, his philanthropy was greeted with disdain from the press, some politicians, and the military and with less than enthusiasm from the Catholic Church, which also had holdings in the area. Perhaps it didn't help that his private ownership—from the Pacific Ocean to the Argentine border—now cut the long thin country of Chile in half. Nowhere in Chilean experience had a foreigner come to spend tens of millions just to give it away to the Chilean public as parklands.

In 1994, Doug married an old friend and fellow conservationist, Kris McDivitt, herself the former CEO of Patagonia. What Doug and Kris have done in Chile, and now in Argentina, is unprecedented anywhere in the world and perhaps at any time in history. They've acquired more than two million acres of private land, created two new national parks, restored degraded farm, grass, forest lands, and rivers, and built hundreds of homes, farm buildings, fences, bridges, gardens, tree nurseries,

Cafe Caleta Gonzalo, an ecotourism facility at a ferry landing in Parque Pumalín, Chile.

apiaries and honey factories, trails, schoolhouses, cafes, cabins, gift shops, ferry landings, campsites, and more.

Now, finally, I was going to see it. Rodrigo Noriega, Doug's pilot, said he would meet us at the small local airport at 8:00 the next morning in a new turbine Cessna 210 on big back country wheels. We packed up and piled in the six-seat single-engine plane, already stuffed three-quarters full of farm supplies, and taxied against the wind to the end of the small runway.

Kris and Doug's house and gardens at Reñihué.

One hundred miles south, we were watching the high snow-capped peaks of the Patagonian Andes out the left side and the coast, small islands, and the blue Pacific out the right side as we flew to Reñihué, the Tompkins' home on a million-acre tract, soon to be Parque Pumalín. From the air, the high mountain lakes, deep green coastal temperate rain forest, waterfalls, and indented shoreline looked virtually identical to the Kitlope and much of coastal British Columbia.

We descended to treetop level and swung over a small bay, looking down on a gorgeous small farm, green fields, inconspicuous buildings all but buried in luxuriant vegetation, a short grass strip widening now out the windshield and hardly a bump as the big turbine engine slowed and we pulled up to a tiedown. We'd arrived at Fundo Pillán, administrative headquarters to the emerging park. We took a quick walk, admiring exquisite facilities designed to blend into the landscape, the largest honey factory in Chile, nurseries for native trees, greeted several bright smiling young Chilean staff, then off we went to meet Doug and

Every fence, every field, every building is classic "design with nature."

Kris. Roaring down hill on the grass strip, pointed straight for the ocean, we were barely off the ground and over a long fjord, when another small farm and perfect grass runway came into view and Rodrigo adeptly swung downwind, and then softly set down on an entry to a world unto itself—Reñihué, the Tompkins' homeplace. At a handmade wooden gate along a wiggly fence of woven saplings, Doug and his wife Kris stood, smiling with a welcoming wave.

What is most interesting to me is the way in which Doug and Kris are restoring degraded farms for the benefit of the

Alerce, the redwood of Chile's coastal temperate rain forest, is an important protected species at Parque Pumalín.

land, revenues, and the well-being of his tenants and employees. They are building a more diverse, more resilient ecosystem, community, and economy. Where there were once eroded and overgrazed pasture, burned forests, and polluted shorelines that were hard-pressed to support a single family with a small herd of cattle, there are now magnificent homes designed exquisitely to fit the landscape, using stone and reclaimed local wood. Where there was once a dusty trail of mud and dirt, there are now winding stone-paved pathways with signs carefully hand carved by local craftsmen. Where there were once a few skinny cows, there are now rows of blueberries, gooseberries, cherry and apple trees, lively painted beehives, draft horses, a few sheep, cattle and chickens, as well as visiting students and agro-tourists from around the world thrilled to be doing voluntary work that gives their lives new meaning. Where there were scarred, burned-over forests with dead trees lying across overgrazed pasture, there are now nurseries of native trees, grown from seed gathered from local sources, nurtured in a seed bed, transplanted to shaded nursery beds, then replanted in the forest. Where there was once a small family of farmers dreaming of the city, there are now young Chilean graduate students of forestry, agriculture, botany, and genetics thrilled to be experimenting with new forms of compost and organic food production. A monoculture has become a polyculture. Where one farm sold one product, it now sells multiple products and services. In Jane Jacobs's terms, this is classic "differentiation growing out of generality"—the evolutionary process that most successfully shapes natural economic development that can indeed grow, adapt, reshape, and restore both land and the full expression of its human and nonhuman inhabitants.

Doug and Kris Tompkins are demonstrating the value of diversity, the benefits of multiple sources of revenue and a variety of job opportunities, the increased ability to respond to stress when an economy is based on healthy, diverse ecosystems in which saving and restoring soil, water, and native plants is as important as spending down both financial and environmental resources.

As Doug puts it: "Some of our work is in pure biodiversity conservation, some of it is in reintroduction of extirpated species, some of it is in reforestation, some of it is in activism, some it is in land conservation, some of it is in agriculture—all in order to try to make a whole view of how one could reshape the economy."

Some have criticized this grand experiment as an act of unusual wealth and arrogance. Is it a feudal system with an autocratic philanthropist forcing his will on the land and its rightful residents, or is it a new model of development? To what extent is this a scalable example of the Earth's realistic capacity to support the most essential human aspirations—true sustainability at last? Only time will tell.

Stone masons, carpenters using salvaged wood from old barns, and carvers work full-time for Tompkins. This is the home of one of his farm managers.

I'm aware, of course, that Doug's experiment is a far cry from the bottom-up approach I've been advocating. It may not be replicable and it may not be the best way to release the energy of local residents. But at a minimum, Doug and Kris have created design with nature, a natural model of what conservation-based development can look like on a scale we've not seen since man's

Kris and Doug Tompkins, at their home in Reñihué, Chile, 2009.

machines have come to dominate the landscape. It's a fairyland of possibility, a vivid picture of the end—if not the means—that should inspire re-creation in as many places and as many forms as there are communities and the lands that support them.

Might Willapa Bay, or other coastal communities in the rain forests of home, be among them?

9

GENERALITIES, DIFFERENTIATION, AND THE BENEFIT OF HINDSIGHT

In Moliere's comedy Le Bourgeois Gentilhomme, *the character Monsieur Jourdain is impressed and grateful to discover that he has been speaking prose for 40 years without even knowing it. With a similar kind of gratitude and hindsight, I'd like to frame a pair of stories within the context of Jane Jacobs's notion of differentiation emerging from generalities. I note that this is hindsight because I didn't become familiar with Jane and her ideas until sometime later. But, as Jane herself noted when she joined our board of directors in 1996, Ecotrust had for years been doing on the ground what she had been writing about in her books. When we helped Mugs Petit find new markets in Portland for fresh wild salmon at three times his dockside price, we were helping Mugs differentiate a generality, separating his particular product—wild, locally caught fish—from all the other salmon, especially farmed salmon, out there in the marketplace. Successful business innovation is essentially the process of creating new and different goods and services for the changing needs and wants of customers. It is difference, not similarity, that creates a competitive advantage. Differentiation is the underlying process of both evolution and economies. Differentiation creates diversity, which creates more resilience—the capability to withstand disturbance.*

"Differentiation emerging from generalities" is a mouthful by any standard, but it's really nothing more than a description of a very simple and universal process that operates in nature and human economic development. To take an industrial example, at the turn of the last century we had cars (the generality), but then sedans, hatchbacks, SUVs, and so on (the differentiations) emerged to fill specific and particular needs. In nature, early mammals had unspecialized feet with five generalized toes with claws; eventually, differentiations emerged such as hooves, wings, flippers, paws, and hands. As Jane Jacobs puts it: "Development is an open-ended process, which creates complexity and diversity, because multiplied generalities are sources of multiplied differentiations—some occurring simultaneously in parallel, others in succession."

When one generalization (in the first of these stories, industrial logging) is replaced by another generalization (selective logging), new and diverse forms of differentiation should naturally emerge.

Clayoquot Sound, British Columbia

I came upon Clayoquot indirectly. On a Lacsa Airlines flight from Miami to a Conservation International board meeting in San José, Costa Rica, in 1988, I met a distracted, professorial-looking entrepreneur named George Patterson. After graduating from Harvard, George had ventured south to Latin America to pursue his love of plants, eventually finding a profitable profession in urban landscaping in Boston and tropical plant nurseries in Florida. We got to talking, discussing our mutual interest in conservation and economic development. George suggested we take up the case for *tagua* or "vegetable ivory," the hard nut from wild palms found in tropical rain forests of South America from which shirt buttons had traditionally been made. If we could convince friends like Yvon Chouinard at Patagonia to use *tagua* buttons on their clothing, we could bring additional value to peasant farmers otherwise tempted to convert rain forests to cattle ranches. About a year later, at a press conference cosponsored by CI, Patagonia announced a new slogan: "Why wear a button that

Clayoquot Sound on the west coast of Vancouver Island, British Columbia. Ecotrust's mapping of coastal temperate rain forests of the world showed that the 600,000-acre Clayoquot watershed contained three of only five watersheds left intact on the island.

says 'Save the Rain Forests' when you can wear one that does." Unfortunately, it turned out that new washing machines ground most of Patagonia's *tagua* buttons to shreds in fairly short order, so instead of saving rain forests Patagonia lost its shirt with their policy of free replacement of defective items. As Yvon admitted later, "That one cost us about a million."

Yvon and I had both fallen for George's infectious enthusiasm for new ideas. Then George called one day in 1989, about the time I was exploring the nature and characteristics of temperate rain forests as a complement to CI's focus on tropical rain forests, and told me about the problems with logging in Clayoquot Sound and that the community had pulled together a "Plan for Sustainable Development" written by someone named Robert Prescott-Allen. He asked if I'd look it over and lend a hand. George's wife, Anne, had grown up in Clayoquot Sound, in Tofino; her father had been a fisherman, her brother ran the local fish plant, and her mother still owned a seaside hotel. George had sold his business in Boston, hurricane Andrew had later destroyed much of his Florida nursery, and he and Anne were moving to Tofino to start

154

a new life. My first thought was, "Oh brother, I'm going to get stuck with another one of George's bright ideas."

Quite the contrary. When I read the plan by Prescott-Allen—an Englishman then living in Victoria who had been one of the authors of the first World Conservation Strategy—I discovered that it was brilliant, one of the most cogent statements of community purpose I'd ever seen. I wanted to meet this man, despite his having just received a pie in the face—literally, from a disgruntled local activist—during the first public review meeting about his draft. Local environmentalists, it turned out, were also bakers and didn't want to hear about "sustainable development." They wanted to stop the logging.

About the same time, the results of Ecotrust and CI's watershed-by-watershed assessment of temperate rain forest priorities in North America was showing that Clayoquot Sound contained three of the five remaining pristine watersheds on Vancouver Island.

Off to Tofino. A remote fishing town on the west coast of Vancouver Island, it's a long haul: a five-hour drive from Victoria, up the east coast of Vancouver Island, then across the island on a winding logging road through vast clear-cuts, the size and audacity of which even a veteran Oregonian had never before seen.

In the early 1990s, Tofino became ground zero for the largest civil disobedience movement in Canadian history. Canadians are slow to rise to protest. In the turmoil of the 1870s, American revolutionaries stayed south, the loyalists fled north. The British Crown still commands respect, and Canadian social welfare provides a substantial safety net in return: universal health care, public education, substantial public service, and government workforce with relatively generous and secure employment and retirement benefits. More than 90 percent of British Columbia is Crown or public land. Canadians generally defer to government policy. So it was amazing when almost 1,000 people were arrested, out of 12,000 who showed up, in protests against large-scale industrial logging of old-growth coastal temperate rain forests on the steep slopes of Clayoquot Sound.

George Patterson and wife, Josie Osborne, with their dog, Griffin.

George introduced me to local environmentalists and Native leaders who were organizing the protests. I shared with them our atlas of coastal temperate rain forests of the world, the detailed inventory of coastal B.C. watersheds, and the news about Clayoquot's relative global importance. It was music to their ears. *Global importance! Burn the logging bridges!*

I chartered a floatplane at Tofino Air to get the bigger view of the entire sound and west coast of Vancouver Island. Clear-cuts went from ridge tops to the ocean's edge for miles. I'll never forget the sight of a large muddy plume below one clear-cut in a beautiful blue mountain lake with waterfalls—a sure-fire national park in most parts of the world.

George was on a wonderful run, busy investing the proceeds of the sale of his business: the purchase of 17 acres on the waterfront for a new home, then a bread-and-breakfast, an industrial warehouse, the local newspaper, a Tofino office building, and the creation of the Clayoquot Biosphere Project, a nonprofit community organization. Planting the roots in "grassroots."

Over the ensuing few years, while logging protests made the front pages and Natives, environmentalists, and business people were being dragged off to jail, Ecotrust quietly set about supporting the efforts for community-based conservation and development. We produced more detailed GIS maps of Clayoquot's environmental, economic, and social conditions. We raised money to bring prominent Chilean, Brazilian, and Mexican journalists to see what Canada was doing at home while their minister of the environment made terrific speeches at the Earth Summit in

Tofino Botanical Gardens.

Rio and happily signed tropical biodiversity and forest conservation treaties. We worked with First Nations on restoring salmon, marine kelp forests, and clam beds. We supported the Clayoquot Biosphere Project and its research programs. We helped draft a proposal for a Clayoquot Sound Biosphere Reserve and introduced the idea to CI board member Francesco di Castri, the French administrator of UNESCO's Man and the Biosphere Program in Paris. We found funding for the construction of a research camp on the Clayoquot River and participated in discussions with government officials and First Nations leaders.

All the while, there was a good long fight afoot with logging interests, well covered on the evening television news. *National Geographic* did an article in September 1990 about temperate rain forests, featuring a multifoldout photograph of a huge clearcut just west of Clayoquot, the infamous Escalante. The Natural Resource Defense Council's Robert Kennedy Jr., showed up to get the many misdeeds of government and industry on the front

Walk of the ancients: old-growth temperate rain forests in Clayoquot Sound.

pages, much to the ire of business and government officials. The Honorable John Fraser, a distinguished Canadian politician and diplomat—one and the same who represented Canada at the Earth Summit—told the press that Clayoquot was a national disgrace. Premier Bill Van der Zalm, a Dutch gardener of the right-wing Social Credit Party and general supporter of business of all and any kind, visited Clayoquot Sound and was quoted in the evening papers saying it would be hard for logging companies to make a bigger mess if they had tried.

There were lots of players, and the story continues to unfold, but Clayoquot Sound may be the most hopeful example of a relatively rapid transition from an industrial to a conservation economy on the West Coast. It is now a UNESCO Man and the Biosphere Reserve with a $12 million endowment for research and education. There's a regional group with local residents and First Nations empowered to make important decisions. A First Nations logging company, Iisaak Forest Resources, controls half of the logging tenure and worked with Ecotrust Canada

"Chicken watching: guaranteed sightings," Tofino Botanical Gardens; infinite differentiations indeed.

on a profitable, ecological forestry mission: small patch-cuts simulating natural wind damage and thinnings instead of huge clear-cuts, income and jobs coming to local people rather than transient logging camps and distant corporations, a style of logging that preserved rather than destroyed salmon spawning beds, and view-sheds that would encourage rather than discourage ecotourism. I created Ecotrust Canada in 1995, run by none other than Ian Gill, one-and-the-same Australian-born journalist, to publicly tell the story of success in the Kitlope and the war in the woods raging in Clayoquot Sound. Ecotrust Canada was designed to support the ongoing work in the bioregion from Alaska to California with additional Canadian staff, funding, and political support for the work in British Columbia. They've made Clayoquot Sound a priority initiative, including Iisaak, the acquisition of historic Cougar Annie's Garden as an educational and conferencing facility, and a wide range of community-development initiatives to support everything from oyster farming, commercial fishing, and ecotourism to working

159

with the Ahousaht First Nations band to build culturally appropriate housing from their own woodlot—bold experiments in
resilience, some more successful than others.

In my first meeting in Tofino, where I shared the global rain
forest atlas, one of the participants noted that if we were successful in stopping industrial logging, there would be no local
jobs left because tourism started in early July and ended after
Labor Day in early September. Today tourism is still prominent,
year-round oyster farming is developing, and local culture is
shifting toward environmental services in all of its differentiating manifestations. Where there was one whale-watching
business there are now seven or eight, some owned by First
Nations. The many great lodges and restaurants in Tofino have
high occupancy rates year-round; they sell winter windstorms
as well as an occasional sunny summer day.

As I've thought about the conditions for even moderate success in Clayoquot Sound, there were several. Leadership and
strategic strength came from First Nations, who had legitimate
claims to continuous use and occupancy of their traditional ter-
ritories, had never signed treaties, and were supported by the
courts, so their concerns had to be taken into account. Numerous
American expats, many of them former Vietnam war protesters
who had fled north to the hippie paradise of Tofino to avoid the
draft, were quick to join the Canadians and First Nations leaders blockading logging roads, burning bridges, and participat-
ing in the noisy debate. There was a big "NO" to the dominant
industrial model of logging and development, which forced a big
"RETHINK." The lines between environment and development
were clearly drawn by the stark contrast between the sound's
beautiful beaches, clear streams, magnificent old-growth forests,
and the scale, intensity, and sheer ugliness of industrial clear-
cutting. The "enemy" was large industrial forest companies with
distant and obscure ownership operating on Crown tree farm
licenses—land "owned" by First Nations and the Canadian public. The protesters were able to embarrass and humiliate both
national and provincial leaders on an international stage. Indeed,

the hypocrisy of the image of Canadian environmental leadership at the Earth Summit versus what they were doing to their own rain forests in much advertised "Super Natural BC" was self-evident. The NDP Provincial government of Michael Harcourt was determined to find a satisfactory compromise around "sustainability." They were getting beat up by all sides, but Harcourt himself was truly committed.

Clayoquot Sound's economic transition is practically a textbook illustration of Jane Jacobs's description of economic development in *The Nature of Economies*. No one in the early 1990s thought there was a future in Clayoquot Sound tourism. It was too remote, the rain and weather was generally dreadful, and the infrastructure was primitive to nonexistent. But once the war over industrial logging was won, the social context for development shifted to an evolutionary, locally based process that was allowed to evolve in new and different ways. Environmental services began to replace natural "resource" products. Some experiments failed, though hopeful, incremental progress across scales of time and space has emerged.

A light went on for me when Chris LeFevre, owner and developer of the Middle Beach Lodge, described his own evolution. Chris built the first lodge with a beautiful, big, open dining area around a huge fire with magnificent views of Pacific waves pounding the rocky beach below. The rooms however, were built assuming people would sleep there but be out and about during the day: a bed, bureau and bathroom, with little space in between. The problem, of course, was that this worked when the weather was good in that brief period called "summer." What Chris realized when he did the second phase of the development was that the rooms needed to be bigger, many with fireplaces and a nice chair in which to read and look out over the pouring rain and pounding shore. In the five minutes of good weather in a typical winter weekend, visitors could dash to the beach, get soaking wet, then return to a cozy room with a view. Annual occupancy went from 30 percent to 90 percent. It is that classic Jane Jacobs "differentiation" from a generalized room to a very specific room suited to particular qualities of place—an evolutionary process similar to adaptation in nature. It's an example of the ways in which local residents were beginning to take ownership and control of their own destiny and fashioning their lives around the realities of local conditions and opportunities.

Among the many crazy ideas of Ecotrust Canada was the acquisition of Cougar Annie's Garden and its eccentric mix of additions by its long-time steward Peter Buckland. Here, a highly differentiated woodshed.

The larger idea of getting economic and natural evolution back in sync, so promising in Clayoquot Sound, is a critical example of a larger strategy for society to address the loss of biological and cultural diversity and create new economic opportunity in the face of global change—a way to more intimately connect the production of environmental goods and services in the country with growing demand from the cities. End the resource curse, by revolution and protest if necessary, get the policy and social context right, and let nature and local, evolutionary economic development take its course.

Copper River Delta, Alaska, at almost one million acres, is one of the largest estuaries in North America.

Copper River, Alaska

Almost 30 years ago, Copper River fishermen grew frustrated with the 60 to 80 cents per pound they were getting for some of the most beautiful large wild Chinook and sockeye salmon in the world. Salmon taste comes in large part from the fat content of the fish, and this has everything to do with the distance the salmon swim upstream to spawn. The Copper River is almost 300 miles long and drains one of the wildest and largest watersheds in the Pacific, producing some three million wild salmon annually. The Copper River Delta is a million-acre wetland inhabited by nesting swans, moose, and wolves. It's 70 miles wide at its mouth, one of the most productive estuaries anywhere, and critical habitat for migrating and nesting waterfowl and the largest populations of migrating shorebirds in the world. In the early 1980s, Copper River fishermen branded their "Copper River wild" salmon, began educating white-table-cloth chefs in Seattle, and soon received closer to $3 per pound for salmon that have become famous in high-end fish markets and

163

restaurants across the United States. and Europe. Again, it was a classic example of moving from commodity to niche product, the process of differentiation that Jane Jacobs described as the heart of both economic and ecological development.

Bill Webber was one of the fishermen who built the Copper River salmon brand. Bill is a progeny of a long Alaskan Tlingit Indian heritage of high-liner fishermen. He is a boat builder, fisher, and fish marketer all rolled into one extraordinary entrepreneur. He lives and works in Cordova, Alaska, and is founder of Gulkana Seafood Direct and Webber Marine & Manufacturing, Inc., builder of the finest aluminum fishing boats on the Copper River flats.

Bill Webber, salmon fisherman, boat builder, and entrepreneur, in his workshop in Cordova.

As boat builder, fisherman, processor, and marketer, he owns the whole "chain of custody" from sea to chef. He knows that quality is king and that everything he can do to maintain the fresh, wild taste of Copper River salmon can be rewarded in the marketplace. So when a salmon rolls over the transom in the gill-net of one of his Copper River "bow pickers," it doesn't it fall flopping wildly on the deck; it is carefully handpicked, slid down a special chute where its gills are cut, beginning the bleeding necessary for optimum flavor, then falls into a saltwater immersion tank, further pressure-bled by hand, cleaned, headed, and put onto layered flake ice. The salmon are processed at sea and delivered to the Cordova airport in 12 to 36 hours. Bill's boat-building adaptations help catch and process a differentiated product for the marketplace that has helped create additional demand for his $250,000 gill-netters.

Copper River fishermen harvest one million salmon annually, so the difference between commodity salmon and branded high-quality salmon means big profits for fishermen in Cordova like Bill Webber.

RJ Kopchak is another Copper River fisherman and long-time Cordova resident. Our introduction in late fall 1989 was auspicious. Danny Vollum had left his de Havilland Beaver float-plane in Anchorage after a moose-hunting trip, and he invited me to fly it home with him before it was buried in snow until spring. It took a day of digging in the ice and preheating the

RJ Kopchak, commercial fisherman, Cordova, Alaska.

engine, but eventually the old nine-cylinder Pratt & Whitney Wasp Jr. engine fired up, and we headed down the foggy coast 500 feet off the deck. The Copper River Delta appeared on the horizon about dusk, and we decided Cordova was our last shot at dry sheets and hot food. I got to poking around town asking questions about fish and wildlife on the Delta and was soon pointed toward an old boat shed where I found Kopchak, a man conspiring to create a local science center in the wake of the *Exxon Valdez* oil spill. A science center would be critical because it would help the fishermen establish baseline data to influence government policy to best preserve the region's natural resources and prevent future oil spills.

The shed was dark. I climbed a ladder to the deck where I could see a faint light in the hold of RJ's bow picker. I shouted down the hold: "Kopchak? My name is Beebe. Can you tell me about your plans for the Prince William Sound Science Center?"

"Yes, and for $50,000 you can be on the board."

That wasn't what I had in mind, but later I did join the board, helped rewrite the by-laws, develop a three-year plan, find a $300,000 start-up grant from the M. J. Murdock Trust, hire full-time staff, and set up a small office in the port captain's old office on a dock in the harbor. I thought a local science center should have a comprehensive GIS database for the entire Prince William Sound and adjacent Copper River watershed, an area of some 25 million acres and just 8,000 full-time residents. The Prince William Sound Science Center worked with public agencies and other private organizations to publish the first big picture book describing the global significance of the *North Gulf of Alaska Ecosystem*.

We also provided a one-year fellowship to a charismatic University of Alaska fisheries extension agent and local fisherman named Rick Steiner. During the trauma of the *Exxon Valdez* oil spill, Rick had become the de facto spokesman for the community in the spotlight of worldwide press. He found some respite in our small office in Portland when he was not in Anchorage or Cordova struggling to identify a cohesive response from the fishing community and local residents affected by the spill. The best that most people could imagine was a huge lawsuit and years of bitter debate.

Rick and I thought we should write up a proposal for a comprehensive early settlement, and spend the money building local capacity to create ecological and social baseline data, habitat protection, and future oil spill prevention and responsiveness. Rick drafted a proposal for a $2 billion settlement and contacted State and Federal authorities, as well as staff of former secretary of the interior and gubernatorial candidate Walter Hickel. The staff bristled and said it was a ridiculous idea, then called Rick the following day to report that Hickel was intrigued and wanted to make settlement a key part of his campaign. He won both the governorship and eventually a $2.2 billion settlement over 10 years to conduct the largest oil spill restoration effort in history. Rick successfully lobbied for several hundred million for protection of private and Alaska Native corporation lands around the coast of the sound, the Kenai Peninsula, and Kodiak Island. Ultimately over 600,000 acres of critical fish and wildlife habitat along the south central coast of Alaska were protected from logging and other damaging industrial activities by this effort. The Science Center, later chaired by Ecotrust VP for Fisheries Edward Backus, has grown to a dozen staff, an annual budget of two to three million dollars, and has become an authoritative voice for marine and natural resource issues in the region. Their expertise has been prominent in the response to the disastrous 2010 BP oil spill in the Gulf of Mexico.

Ecotrust, meanwhile, has acquired a few scattered private holdings in the vast expanse of public lands with the hopes of helping to prevent oil and gas, coal, road building, and logging on the Copper River Delta. RJ Kopchak was the lead Ecotrust project manager in Cordova for five years. We employ four full-time staff and have been at it now for 20 years in Prince William Sound and the Copper River ecosystem. I sometimes wonder what we have accomplished and where we are headed.

Cordova harbor, home to one of the few viable remaining fishing fleets in the United States. The Prince William Sound Science Center is in the upper right.

Our hope was to help local residents maintain the fisheries and therefore the fishing economy, prevent inappropriate development, and help provide permanent protection to the Copper River Delta. The challenge has involved building sufficient momentum in a population of just a few thousand people in an area the size of New England.

With few scattered exceptions, fisheries management worldwide has been an unmitigated disaster. Since the beginning of large-scale industrial fishing almost 100 years ago, one marine species and population after another has been overfished to commercial and almost biological extinction. Atlantic cod was no exception. Despite warehouses full of scientific evidence and the well-meaning speeches of fisheries ministers for decades, an extraordinarily rich and abundant population of cod and their dependent fishers from New England to Europe all but disappeared over a decade ago.

Alaska is a hopeful exception. With all seven species of salmon across the north Pacific from Korea, Japan, China, and the Russian Far East, right down the West Coast from Alaska to California, the pattern is clear. Wild salmon are declining in both numbers and population diversity from south to north on both sides of the Pacific along with their attendant fishers. Some 500 million to perhaps a billion wild, healthy salmon that populated the Pacific for millions of years are being replaced by smaller, more expensive, and not always healthy hatchery and farm fish. Free salmon are being replaced by expensive salmon. Where fishery managers see fish counts declining, they see primarily a numbers problem. So they respond with a numbers solution: dump more industrial hatchery fish into the rivers and oceans at taxpayer expense. But, as ethnographer Gary Paul Nabhan has said, species extinction is not a problem of declining numbers, it is a problem of the species becoming disconnected from its environment. Diverse, natural habitat in both land and sea, and their intimate relations with salmon streams produce diversity of life histories of populations of salmon. Hatcheries, on the other hand, are a 130-year-old experiment that has failed. Additionally, when we simplify rivers with rip-rap, straightening, dams, pollution, sedimentation, water withdrawals, irrigation, streamside habitat destruction, overgrazing, and insensitive logging, we reduce the complexity and diversity of connections and relationships that then reduce the productivity of salmon streams. Restore that natural complexity of changing stream channels, wetlands, and riparian vegetation, and salmon will restore themselves. It is cheaper, faster, and more effective than trying to replace nature with our expensive and often counterproductive technology.

Salmon farms are even worse than the arrogance of hatcheries. Worldwide, they have introduced a vast array of environmental problems and have had a damaging impact on wild salmon. We should get them all out of the ocean everywhere they occur and vastly reduce the hatcheries to a few that could be helpful in jump-starting salmon recovery where they have been entirely extirpated. The fisheries challenge is to stop the multiple sources of degradation, get out of nature's way, and let ocean and stream ecosystems recover. Jim Lichatowich, a leading salmon biologist, Ecotrust board member, and author of *Salmon Without Rivers*, says it as clearly and succinctly as anyone: "We fail because we have succeeded with our model; replace nature with technology."

So in the few places left on earth, like the Kitlope River in British Columbia and the Copper River in Alaska, where undisturbed natural systems still rule the roost, it is particularly important to learn how nature does it, protect those processes, and model our fisheries practices on nature's model. That is why Bill Webber and RJ Kopchak's model of protecting habitat and wild runs of chinook and sockeye salmon—harvesting a modest annual increment of what nature produces, then differentiating their products to optimize value—is so precious and so promising.

The traditional environmental approach in the Copper River would be to launch a campaign to save the Copper River top-down via national wilderness or park legislation as was done for, say, the Arctic National Wildlife Refuge in the 1950s. Ecotrust has a different approach to conservation. We're trying to build on the distinct environmental and cultural characteristics of the region, which create very particular, differentiated economic opportunities for the people who live there. RJ and his successive team are supporting a growing network of local leaders: Native Americans, fishermen, scientists, and just plain local folks. Support them, network them, and help tell their stories. Our hope is to build on a self-organizing system, and support bold, not-afraid-to-fail experiments—a more natural and powerful approach to resilience than traditional top-down command and control. We will constantly adapt and evolve as we explore what works and what doesn't.

The Arctic National Wildlife Refuge on Alaska's North Slope is a protected area resulting from years of environmental campaigning. Despite that, however, much of society has been shouting, "Drill, drill, drill!" Society does what society thinks. We won't save the Arctic National Wildlife Refuge until we move our mental model from industrial command-and-control development to a natural model, one that recognizes the human species as part of a larger community of life.

The Ecotrust Board floating down Copper River in 2003.

10

THE FIRST ENVIRONMENTAL BANK:
A New Take on "Green"

I stated earlier that the idea of starting Ecotrust hatched full-blown like a phoenix around a campfire in the Kitlope. This is fanciful, of course, though the idea of helping local people meet their social and economic needs while preserving their environment was central from the beginning and remains so today. I'd learned in Mexico and Costa Rica that understanding the culture and constraints of local people was no small assignment, and I was later to learn in Willapa Bay that local energy can often produce as much negative strife as positive change. But I see no way to integrate conservation and development other than building on the cultural and economic traditions of local communities. For one thing, local people can't afford to see their environment as an object to be either exploited or saved. Their economic and social well-being is interwoven with the environment in such a way that either developing or saving their environment means developing or saving themselves in that environment. It means conserving and restoring the natural resources on which their lives and livelihoods depend. It means building on the natural competitive advantage of the very particular qualities of the bioregion.

As to how to go about helping them do this, I had only the foggiest notion. From the start, I envisioned Ecotrust as a catalyst and broker,

172

but I never in my wildest dreams envisioned starting an environmental bank. That idea came later—again, around a campfire. Campfires, like dudes, are good for conservation.

ShoreBank Pacific, Ilwaco, Washington

Paul Benoit is the city manager of Astoria, a small coastal Oregon town at the mouth of the Columbia River with a long and proud history. Astoria was the first white settlement west of the Mississippi, a fur trading post established in 1811 by John Jacob Astor of New York. It was to be Astor's stepping stone to China and global dominance of the fur trade. Lewis and Clark arrived here on a stormy day in November 1805, and spent a rainy winter at nearby Fort Clatsop.

There was one part of Astoria that did not make Paul Benoit proud. On the east end of town, on the banks of the mighty river, was Oregon's worst brownfield site. Seventeen acres of greasy, dead pond—the last remains of a bankrupt plywood mill, the

Paul Benoit at the Mill Pond, Astoria, Oregon.

final stage of more than 100 years of sawing the huge old-growth logs of the surrounding forest, a vestige of a logging boom in an industrial age.

In 1998, Oregon's Department of Environmental Quality offered the city matching funding to clean up the site, an estimated total of $1.5 million. Paul thought that the cleanup and redevelopment of the old mill pond was a critical part of turning the historic town around rather than have it go the way of so many former coastal boomtowns, just another roadside attraction of cheap hotels, fast food, decaying streets, car bodies over the bank, and disenchanted youth doing everything possible to get out of town. However, Astoria didn't have $750,000 to match the state's offer to restore the Mill Pond. They went to the local community bank, the Bank of Astoria. The local bankers were not impressed: cleaning up a superfund site? Not on your life! Paul was getting desperate when he ran into John Berdes at ShoreBank Enterprise Pacific across the bridge in Ilwaco, Washington, who said he might be able to help. What is ShoreBank Enterprise Pacific? How do they, in Ecotrust's now-familiar parlance, "release the energies of local residents"? That's actually a pretty good story.

The Astoria Mill Pond, brownfield-turned-greenfield and prime residential community on the banks of the Columbia River.

It starts early in 1991 in Edmonton, Alberta, where I was giving a paper at the North American Wildlife Conference on what we called "conservation-based development in the rain forests of home." Alana Probst, Ecotrust's director of economic development (her business card actually said "Queen of EcoDevo") had created the Oregon Marketplace, which strove to build Oregon businesses through "import substitution," the process of doing better at home what previously had been done elsewhere. Alana became friends with Jane Jacobs, who said that ShoreBank—the country's leading community development financial institution, headquartered in Chicago—was the only bank she liked. I knew something about conserving the environment and was committed to Native American and First Nations communities, but knew little or nothing about economic development. ShoreBank committed itself to "social equity," creating opportunities for low- and moderate-income residents of what they called "disinvested communities."

From a hotel room in Edmonton, I picked up the phone and called Mary Houghton, president and one of the four founders of ShoreBank. I mentioned Alana and Jane Jacobs, so she took the call. I told her we had started an organization devoted to the "triple bottom line," the improvement of environmental, economic, and social equity in the coastal temperate rain forest bioregion from Alaska to California. ShoreBank had the "equity" and "economy," I had the "environment" and "equity." "Maybe we should work together and pursue the three Es: equity, economy, and environment? Then we'd have a whole-systems approach." I invited her to join the Ecotrust board and, only the Creator knows why, she accepted right then and there.

Then it got more interesting.

One of my last hurrahs at CI was taking some Rockefeller Foundation trustees around Mexico to explore funding opportunities. In the end, I apparently wasn't very persuasive, and they decided not to do conservation in Mexico. Perhaps they were feeling sympathetic after having taken so much time, so they gave CI $75,000 to do a series of workshops to explore large-scale ecosystem conservation and development throughout the

Americas. It may not have been precisely what the Rockefeller Foundation had in mind, but this turned out to be four week-long float trips down Idaho's Middle Fork of the Salmon River in the Frank Church Wilderness Area, trips built around different themes: science, economic development, policy, and the nature of complex adaptive systems.

The venue was so appealing that we attracted top people from Brazil, Mexico, the United States, and Canada. Over breakfast, lunch, and dinner around a campfire on the beach, beside the pristine green water of the Middle Fork, deep in a spectacular steep canyon under old-growth ponderosa pine, each participant gave a talk to the group. Then we floated, walked, kayaked, hot-springed, bird-watched, and fly-fished our way down the river, each time mixing the 12 to 15 guests. A writer recorded and shared the evolving discourse, and as the fast river slowed, the canyon opened up in drier country and everyone began to relax and settle in with one another. A synthesis gradually emerged into what was eventually published as a four-part annual series called "The Middle Fork Conference."

Middle Fork Conference, Salmon River, Idaho. Mary Houghton and Jane Jacobs were helping to think about how to start the world's first environmental bank.

So, when the economic development–themed raft trip came around, I invited Mary Houghton, who by that time was on the Ecotrust board. Rafting down wild rivers is not the first thing you think of when you meet Mary Houghton in ShoreBank's headquarters on the south side of Chicago. But this rafting trip was a board responsibility, and Mary is game for anything different, especially new ideas with interesting people.

We were sitting around a campfire on about day three in that summer of 1993, deep into discussing how we might unleash the unlimited creativity and energy of local residents to create economic opportunity and fuel ecosystem restoration. Mary looked up at one point and said, "Let's start a bank!" So we did.

Not right there around the campfire, of course. It would take several years of planning, almost monthly two-day meetings between the senior staff of Ecotrust and ShoreBank, and some excruciatingly difficult fundraising from coast to coast. But after all this, we created a business plan and offered documents for "ShoreBank Pacific Corporation, the First Environmental Bank," a wholly owned subsidiary bank holding company of the parent ShoreBank in Chicago. Under the ShoreBank Pacific holding company, we detailed three subsidiary affiliates: ShoreBank Pacific, a regulated, *de novo* commercial bank designed to make loans to small- and medium-sized businesses in both urban and rural markets in the coastal Pacific Northwest; ShoreBank Enterprise Pacific, a nonprofit "community development financial institution" designed to support small and emerging businesses and organizations that didn't have the credit history or collateral to allow them to go to existing banks; and, finally, a real estate company designed to support green development with equity and debt.

And, of course, our plan was to headquarter all this in Ilwaco, Washington, an all-but-abandoned fishing town in Washington State, on the north banks of the mouth of the Columbia River, population 800—and declining. I say "of course" because this was entirely consistent with both ShoreBank and Ecotrust policy to always do the most difficult thing in the most challenging way imaginable.

177

One immediate challenge was the fact that what we wanted to do—start a *de novo* bank in the state of Washington—was illegal without a charter, and we didn't have one. In the end, we somehow managed to persuade U.S. Bank to donate an unused charter—an unheard-of gesture on the part of one bank to a potential competitor. U.S. Bank has been a great partner ever since.

But becoming legal was far from our only challenge. When I went around to explain our plans to prospective funders and investors, I drew a record number of unabashed, disbelieving, blank stares. Fortunately, Mary's colleague Ron Grzywinski, the chairman of ShoreBank, usually traveled with me, dressed very much like a banker, and with ShoreBank's history and reputation we eventually won the day. Ron and I raised almost $10 million in capital and several million in operating support. For the nonprofit we could raise both loan capital and operating support from charitable donations. For bank capital we offered common equity voting and/or nonvoting shares in ShoreBank Corporation, the parent, and stipulated that capital would be 100 percent downstreamed as initial capital to ShoreBank Pacific. The beauty of bank holding companies, Ron would explain, is a largely unrecognized clause of the banking act that allows them to use their resources for the well-being of the residents of the communities in which they work. It was a broad interpretation rarely used by other bankers. So, in effect, the holding company structure and board orchestrated the activities of a potentially diverse array of subsidiary commercial and public service entities toward common purpose while raising money from diverse sources: private equity capital, FDIC-insured deposits, governmental and charitable grants, and earned income and profits. Ron's speech always revolved around the establishment of a "permanent development institution," one that grew and was self-funded.

Several foundations were persuaded that they should make grants to Ecotrust so it could invest in ShoreBank, rather than investing directly themselves. Thus Ecotrust ended up with an investment of $3.5 million in ShoreBank, almost five percent of

Ron Grzywinski, chairman and one of the four founders of ShoreBank, board member of Ecotrust and Ecotrust Canada.

the voting stock at the time, as well as having board positions and an ongoing partnership.

Leverage is an important idea and banks are particularly good at it, sometimes too good at it, despite enormous regulatory constraints. Banks can raise deposits in proportion to capital at a ratio of roughly 10:1. So $10 million in capital becomes $100 million in deposits, which in turn are lent at a loan-deposit ratio of as much as 8:1. So $10 million becomes $80 million in loans, and of course the spread between the cost of deposits and the interest rate on loans generates the bank's earnings and its ability to grow. It's a sort of green alchemy that is hard to reproduce in a nonprofit environmental structure.

In 1995, we started the Northwest work with ShoreBank Enterprise Pacific, the nonprofit. It seemed like the lowest risk but sharpest edge of the plough. Since we weren't putting insured deposits at risk, we could experiment and make all the

179

dumb loans we wanted as far as the regulators were concerned. Ecotrust incorporated the nonprofit, provided start-up financial and administrative support as well as grant money, and converted an old fish cannery on the Ilwaco harbor front into an office. On day one, we cleaned some remaining sturgeon off the floor and started the restoration. I think Bob the Sturgeon's stuffed remains still decorate the wall.

At the time, ShoreBank Enterprise had a total revolving loan fund of $2.5 million, hard-won capital that we raised crisscrossing the country for three years. Our policy was not to loan more than 10 percent of the fund in any single transaction. So when Paul Benoit came asking for $750,000 for a brownfield redevelopment, I was skeptical; it seemed like a great way to dig a giant financial hole right from the get-go. But my colleagues were persuasive. We built this institution to take calculated risks, they argued, listing the reasons we should make the loan. We invest in entrepreneurs and local leaders with a long-term commitment to place. Astoria is the largest community in our service area and it's facing a critical turning point. Many people, including prominent politicians, will let any fast, cheap development come to town on the promise of a few jobs, but a growing minority of citizens see a different future and have a thoughtful, carefully orchestrated plan to reconnect the waterfront with the downtown and Victorian neighborhoods on the surrounding hill, a narrow gauge railroad for public transportation, new sidewalks, a maritime museum, and a renovated Liberty Theater. These are the very people we need to help, and this is the moment in time when we need to step up and do it. Before they were through I was beginning to feel like the Bob Jenkins of the group, and I didn't like it. But in the end we blew off the loan policy, something a nonprofit is uniquely able to do, and made a commitment to Paul Benoit.

He delivered in more ways than we could have imagined. The state DEQ helped clean up the Astoria Mill Pond, the city sent out a request for redevelopment proposals, and Art Demuro of Venerable Properties in Portland won the bid—$1.3 million for 17 acres on the banks of the Columbia River in a beautiful, small historic town. With Enterprise's commitment, ShoreBank Pacific, our commercial bank, followed, and ultimately the Bank of Astoria joined in as well. The U.S. Environmental Protection Agency recognized the project as a leading national example of brownfield redevelopment with its Phoenix Award.

Where there was once oily water leaking into the Columbia, a lifeless, weedy pond surrounded by rusting metal, hydrocarbon-soaked soil, an industrial eyesore and stain on the city's reputation, there is now a clean, clear pond replanted with native vegetation, grebes, ducks, and loons, and three dozen smart, affordable wood homes appropriate to the community. It was a great example of public-private, for-profit/nonprofit collaboration in which local, state, and federal governments, environmentalists, planners, developers, and social activists worked together to create something real and meaningful at a very local level, but in a way that had national, perhaps global, application. Paul Benoit's tenacity and leadership helped turn the whole city around and point it to a hopeful future.

Paul Benoit's story is only one of many. Dave Nesbit, the owner of Goose Point Oyster, is both grower and processor of a variety of oyster products and has been one of the more entrepreneurial and innovative oystermen in Willapa Bay. His plant is on the east side of Willapa at the mouth of the Niawakum River and employs 35, mostly Hispanic, workers. Dave has had his challenges building the business: the whimsy of Pacific storms, acquiring sufficient beds to produce most of his own product, and finding a banker that understood the business of oystering. John Berdes of ShoreBank Enterprise came to his rescue—not once but many times, when Dave was either saving what he had, developing a new product, or looking for new markets. Dave will quickly tell you that without ShoreBank he might not have made it. There are hundreds of small businesses on the Oregon and Washington coasts that might say the same.

Today, 15 years after its founding, ShoreBank Enterprise Cascadia—our name after merging with the Cascadia revolving

Dave Nisbet, owner of Goose Point Oyster, Niawakum River, Willapa Bay.

loan fund in Seattle—has almost $30 million in loan funds from charitable and government sources. It manages over $100 million in New Markets Tax Credits, employs 40 staff in nine offices, and generates over 70 percent of revenue from loan interest and earned income. To date, ShoreBank Enterprise has made over 450 loans to small businesses and community organizations in coastal Oregon and Washington. ShoreBank Pacific and Enterprise teamed up on a new, green, 10,000-square-foot headquarters building on the harbor that has had a demonstrable effect on the restoration of Ilwaco.

Perhaps the best thing we did was to hire some smart people and get out of the way. Mike Dickerson came from a background as both park guard and community developer; John Berdes came from low-income housing. They work well together and share a deep commitment to addressing poverty as well the environment. And they work nonstop. John and Mike participated with the Ford Foundation on an international team from Africa, Asia, Latin America, and the United States, looking at the integration of strategies to improve environmental conditions while addressing poverty. They also teamed up with the city of Portland on low-income housing energy improvements and with the Bill and Melinda Gates Foundation on septic improvements to clean up Puget Sound.

Dave Williams, a former physics teacher and businessman from a sixth-generation Willapa Bay oyster family, runs ShoreBank Pacific. He has grown the commercial bank from a tiny office in a trailer house adjacent to the old fish cannery in Ilwaco into a profitable bank with $250 million in assets, over $175 million in "Eco-Deposits" from some 3,000 depositors in every state in the United States and 10 countries abroad, and a handsome renovated office in downtown Portland. Dave has become an important spokesman for the growing idea of "green banking" throughout the country. The last quarter of 2008—the year in which U.S. banking led the world into the worst financial crisis since the Great Depression—he completed his tenth quarter with growing profits and ended the year with $1.3 million in net earnings.

Ecotrust had an effect on the entire ShoreBank holding company as well. The original community bank quickly understood that an interest in the environment did not mean only salmon and old-growth forests out West. Why make loans to mom-and-pop rehabbers of multifamily housing if the heat all goes out the window, the residents are breathing toxic paint, and the water is still coming through lead pipes? ShoreBank adopted the triple-bottom-line mission everywhere it works. By the end

Dave Williams, ShoreBank Pacific CEO, in Portland, Oregon.

of 2008, ShoreBank had leveraged our original $10 million in new capital to over $1 billion in conservation loans.

Mary and her colleagues have grown ShoreBank from $750 million in 1991 to $2.5 billion in assets in 2009. It's the largest community financial development institution in the United States, with 11 subsidiaries operating in the United States and 50 countries abroad. In 2008, ShoreBank raised almost $30 million in new capital at a time when CitiBank and Bank of America were getting federal bailouts from Washington. The economic crisis hit particularly hard in ShoreBank's low-income markets in Chicago, Detroit, and Cleveland, and banking isn't much fun right now. In 2010, ShoreBank has raised over $157 million, is itself seeking federal matching funds, and is struggling to return to profitability despite 20 to 30 percent unemployment rates in the communities they serve. The ultimate test of resilience at a time of severe stress is yet to come, but the general model should be one that differentiates around the world as the need for creative capitalism grows. By "creative capitalism," we mean businesses that both make money and alleviate poverty, both of which are worthy goals but neither of which can be accomplished without addressing the environment as well—the life-support systems upon which we all depend.

ShoreBank Pacific and ShoreBank Enterprise Cascadia headquarters in Ilwaco, Washington.

11

FROM COUNTRY TO CITY:
Creating a Living Building

While we were helping to get ShoreBank Enterprise and ShoreBank Pacific underway, the famous urbanist Jane Jacobs joined Ecotrust's board and we began to think more seriously about the relationships between city and country. Capital, jobs, and technology, after all, are created mostly in cities. As Ecotrust advisor Stewart Brand of Whole Earth Catalogue *fame points out in his new book* Whole Earth Discipline, *everyone seems to be moving to town. In 1800, cities were home to three percent of the world's population; in 1900, 14 percent; by 2007, over 50 percent. The world is urbanizing, and Stewart argues that this relieves the pressure on the natural environment in the country while creating innovation in the dense and youthful cities.*

Our work until then had been in small coastal communities like Cordova, Alaska; Kitamaat and Tofino, British Columbia; and Willapa Bay, Washington, where we were trying to help local residents improve economic opportunity while protecting and restoring unique forest and salmon habitat. While we tried to help forge connections between rural supplies of environmentally sound goods and services, we had not tried as hard to stimulate demand in the cities. It was supply push more than demand pull. Jane Jacobs encouraged us to think more explicitly about the city—a thought that comes slowly to environmentalists whose main concerns are for biodiversity and ecosystem health.

About the same time, however, I was thinking that Ecotrust needed to do more about building its own financial capital. We were eager to become more self-sufficient, address our own long-term economic health, and grow our working endowment, the Natural Capital Fund. We had fixed up a nice office space in an old mill on the Willamette River waterfront in downtown Portland. Our landlord, Naito Properties, controlled some $150 million in northwest Portland properties that they had acquired and restored in the largely abandoned parts of skid row that most commercial developers had ignored. When our lease was not extended because our architect neighbors needed to expand into our space, my old advisor Jack Vaughn, our board chairman at the time, replied, "Portland Community College rents; Harvard owns."

And there was one more thing: we had a terrific young golden retriever, Bumble Beebe, who liked coming to the office with me. I was told on the elevator one day by another tenant that Albers Mill was a proper office building and that dogs weren't allowed. That settled it. In 1997, I began to look around for a building we could buy. Ecotrust would figure out how to create urban demand for rural environmental goods and services and become owner instead of tenant. And I could bring Bumble to work.

The Jean Vollum
Natural Capital Center,
Portland, Oregon

Ecotrust's offices in Albers Mill were directly across from the Union Pacific Railroad station. The railroad had controlled some 35 blocks of northwest Portland. The waterfront shipyards, docks, and railroad yards had been the center of shipping and distribution of the goods of a developing industrial frontier. But by the early 1980s, trucks were hauling much that had earlier been shipped and railroaded. The 35 blocks of railroad freight yards were largely abandoned. Downtown redevelopment had not yet crossed north of Burnside Avenue into what is now known as the Pearl District. Old multistory warehouses, empty railroad yards, and raised street overpasses diverted traffic around or over most of the area.

An architect-contractor friend named Lindley Morton and I had talked about doing something together. One day Lindley called. "Spencer, I think you'd better come look at something with me," he said. He took me but 10 blocks from Albers Mill to a two-story 1890 warehouse on a full 200-by-200-foot city block between Northwest Ninth and Tenth Avenues and Irving and Johnson Streets. It was still used as a warehouse, although small second-story offices were leased to a few starving artists. It was 70,000 square feet, including a full basement. The original half block had fine architectural features largely obscured by layers of peeling gray paint. Blackberries were growing from the roof, and the brick cornice was crumbling. It was a pile of leaky, unreinforced masonry sitting atop an active seismic zone in abandoned railroad yards where few even dared to walk.

Lindley went on: "Two-and-a-half million dollars for the whole block. Some developers bought it from the aging owner but they are divided and in trouble, so I made an offer. It's too big for me alone. What do you think?"

"Let's do it," I said. "But I'd better go talk with Jean Vollum. She may be the only other person I know who just might think this could be good idea."

Over tea, I described our idea to Jean. Since our first raft trip down the Sandy River in 1975, the Vollums had been good supporters. Jean had helped with important projects like Sycan Marsh, the Snake River Birds of Prey, the development of The Nature Conservancy International, then Conservation International, the creation of Ecotrust and some of our early projects. The Vollums had made very substantial and generally anonymous gifts to Portland schools and universities for arts and crafts, music, scientific research, and a magnificent Alvar Aalto library at a Benedictine abbey in the Willamette Valley. But they had not made a seven-figure gift for the environment.

Jean was persuaded that Ecotrust needed an endowment to endure, that the Northwest environment deserved major support, and that a building bearing her name just might be a lasting expression of her interest in an experimental approach to figuring things out. I suggested we aim to "repurpose a warehouse designed to distribute the goods of an industrial economy into a marketplace for the ideas, goods, and services of a conservation economy." She may have been the only person on earth who would buy such a pretentious idea. Jean committed $2.5 million for the

Jean Vollum. A long way from our first phone conversation in 1975.

purchase of the whole block contingent on our ability to raise another $10 million for redevelopment.

"Repurpose a warehouse designed to distribute the goods of an industrial economy into a marketplace for the ideas, goods and services of a conservation economy." That was the most succinct, single sentence we could invent to describe our purpose for the "Jean Vollum Natural Capital Center." The only problem was that virtually no one had the vaguest idea what that meant.

My colleague on the project was Bettina von Hagen, our vice-president for the Natural Capital Fund, the same inspired recovering banker who helped us develop ShoreBank Pacific. Bettina shared the basic Ecotrust ingredients for success in spades: a high tolerance for ambiguity and a low coefficient of boredom.

The Natural Capital Center not long after its construction in 1890 in northwest Portland. Here it is the United States Steel Products Company.

McCracken Warehouse as it looked in February, 1998, when Ecotrust purchased it. The dark patch on the cornice was the result of bricks falling onto the sidewalk.

A break came when we pulled together a group of people who knew a lot more about development than we did. We invited an old friend, Stewart Brand, who had just published a book called *How Buildings Learn*, to a design charette. Stewart said we had a choice between two alternatives, both good and commendable but completely different and mutually exclusive: "demonstration project or laboratory."

By "demonstration project," Stewart Brand meant showcasing all the latest green technology: gray water systems (using rain water to flush toilets), solar photovoltaics on the roof, the latest insulation and energy-saving HVAC systems, low-toxicity paints, and recycled carpeting, etc. It was a good thing to do but would be expensive and outdated in a few short years. It was the hardware solution, more goods than services.

But I was looking for a social system, software designed on a natural model. "Laboratory" meant a place that was constantly experimenting, an evolving mix of tenants, where people would

The Jean Vollum Natural Capital Center after completion in late 2001.

interact spontaneously and test new ideas. It sounded much more like the dynamic "marketplace" idea we said we were trying to create. Stewart's example was the MIT Media Lab, an old metal military barracks with wood floors and moveable walls in Cambridge, Massachusetts. It was such a dump no one cared if you nailed things to the wall, dragged old furniture across the hall for a makeshift conference room, or played mumbly peg with jack knives on the floor. "Old buildings produce new ideas, new buildings produce old ideas," said Stewart. And the MIT Media Lab lived true, producing some of the most creative initiatives of the information age.

So laboratory—or, more precisely, *evolution*—was design-with-nature principle number one for the Jean Vollum Natural Capital Center. The other two were *diversity* and *connectedness*, principles also derived from healthy ecosystems.

Most people assumed that our intention was to build a center for environmental nonprofits. I couldn't imagine anything less interesting. We knew our friends the environmentalists and would learn little new from each other from proximity that we hadn't already from familiarity. We wanted a diversity of tenants, both retail and office, for profit and nonprofit, public and private. We wanted the giant sucking sound of retail to bring a wide range of people to the marketplace and mix it up with workplace in the offices on the two floors above. Diversity, but with limits. We didn't want just one of everything, but clusters of tenants around particular themes of interest: social finance, forestry, fisheries, green building, food and farms, and the outdoors. Around a social finance "cluster," for example, we had ShoreBank Pacific, with FDIC insured Eco-Deposits, low-risk, low-return investments that would be turned into loans to local businesses trying to improve the triple bottom line; plus the Lemelson Foundation making grants for innovation worldwide; plus Progressive Investments, a socially responsible investment firm managing equity for high-net-worth and social and environmentally motivated investors. And, of course, Ecotrust with experienced staff able to help other organizations gain access to charitable grants and social capital.

Diversity, difference, differentiation: in Jane Jacobs's words, "differentiation emerging from generality" is the core process underlying both ecological and economic development.

But every big downtown office building has diversity, in most cases more than we could create in just 50,000 square feet of restored above-grade space. The critical ingredient was connectedness.

Nature has no impermeable surfaces; resources flow through ecosystems and are shared, stored, restored, and recycled constantly. The interesting places in nature are eco-centers where large amounts of food or water or other scarce resources are relatively abundant, such as grizzly bears, gulls, and ravens feeding on spawning salmon. And ecotones, the interface of distinct habitat types or landscapes where species mix: the forest edge of a meadow, stream banks, an estuary or watering hole in dry country. That is where the action and interaction is: where individuals meet, mate, reproduce, eat and are eaten, where populations evolve, where both positive and negative feedback loops occur—and some are tossed from the gene pool.

Early in redevelopment, from the northwest.

West face under redevelopment. The steel stairs are part of seismic reinforcement.

So we set about designing open space: large hallways; an atrium; an open rooftop around, naturally, a fireplace; a wide loading dock where people could sit outside; conference rooms of every possible size and configuration; mezzanines for hiding; and a public trail connecting them all, winding from the first and second floors up outside stairs to the roof-top terrace.

Open and permeable design conflicted with two important things. One was cost. The Natural Capital Center was designed to make money. It was an investment of our Natural Capital Fund and was supposed to generate earnings to support Ecotrust operations. It was a commercial enterprise, and the expense of repurpose and restoration was so high there was little budget for extras. Every common space was potentially rentable space and would be subject to a load charge to tenants that had to stay within reasonable standards.

The other challenge was creating sufficient private space for security, brand identity of the distinct tenants, and quiet offices where people could talk on the phone and fuss with computers.

Ironically, the developer we hired was the landlord that kicked us out of Albers Mill, Bob Naito. He was the best, along with imaginative architects from Holst—John Holmes and Jeff Stuhr—who were just young enough to want to do the job but do it for nickels, and Bob Walsh, an experienced contractor whom I had known all my life and whose competence and integrity I trusted more than a competitive bidding process. Walsh and Naito saved our naive rear ends, but we drove them all crazy with our design-with-nature criteria, our insistence on saving all the original materials, including the old-growth Douglas fir floors on the first floor that the city tried to make us cover with plywood, and the fireplace on the roof nobody believed was legal. Walsh put a young supervisor, Carrington E. Barrs, "CEB," on the job right out of the University of Washington's green building masters program.

We bought the block in 1998, began redevelopment early in 2000, and had a big party to open for business on Friday, September 6, 2001, just five days before 9/11. One way or another, Bettina and I raised $12 million from grants, foundation program related loans, historic tax credits, and $3.7 million in commercial debt. Bettina personally recruited virtually every tenant, screening them for true shared values, diversity, and authentic experience in one of our targeted economic clusters.

I once told my fishing companion Yvon Chouinard that I was considering buying an old building and fixing it up. He said "Good. If you do that I'll put a Patagonia store in it." And he did, the largest Patagonia store in the world, half of the first floor, an anchor retail tenant without which I am not sure we could have made it. At the opening party Chouinard told a large crowd that the environmentally most responsible thing was to buy used clothes at Goodwill, not new clothes at Patagonia. The same with buildings: reuse the old ones.

195

Shortly after completion. Portland City Streetcar opened about the same time.

Other tenants include the city of Portland's Office of Sustainable Development, which manages the city's programs in recycling, energy, green building, and climate change; the Wild Salmon Center, which promotes wild Pacific salmon conservation throughout its range from Korea to the Russian Far East, Alaska to California; Cascadia Green Building Council, Bob Naito's development consulting business; ClimateSmart, the E3 network of progressive economists from around the world; Sustainable Harvest, which sells fair-trade, shade-grown, organic coffee from small coffee farmers' co-ops around the world; Progressive Asset Management, which developed a $350-million socially responsible investment fund; Upstream 21, which is a part of Progressive, promoting private equity deals for small forest-products businesses; Trout Mountain Forestry, a small forestland management consulting business; and the Bill Healy Foundation, supporting education and the environment in Oregon and Hawaii. The Pearl Health Clinic provides holistic health care, while two food service businesses on the first floor provide coffee and healthy, inexpensive, relatively fast seasonal

196

food at the Laughing Planet Cafe and Hot Lips Pizza. And, of course, Ecotrust with some 50 staff working in fisheries, forestry, food and farms, knowledge systems, and support to Native American and First Nations throughout the bioregion.

The Billy Frank Jr. Conference Center is 1,800 square feet and honors the Martin Luther King of Northwest Indians. Billy Frank has been fighting for tribal fishing rights for almost 60 years, and we named the conference facility for him as an honored Northwest citizen and activist. The Conference Center hosts more than 500 events a year, everything from Pearl Rotary and church services to yoga, dog obedience training, birthday celebrations, and every kind of green-build, local food, sustainable forestry, nonprofit training class, and corporate planning conference under the Northwest oyster sky.

Seven years later, almost three million visitors have come to the Natural Capital Center from all over the world. When you come in the main entry, there is a water fountain on the right under a painting of Mt. Hood and the Sandy River's Bull Run River watershed, a reminder of where our great water

The atrium under construction.

comes from. One day visitors are grade school students or architecture grads learning what it means to build green. Another day, they are 30 mayors from Chinese cities taking the tour of Portland and some of its highlights, or Oregon Congressman Earl Blumenauer giving a tour to Nancy Pelosi, or Nike having a planning retreat.

People are allowed to bring their dogs, which seems to have special attraction. Some just come with their pets at their sides, get a cup of coffee, and tune in to one of Portland's first free wireless Internet connections, and treat the place like an office. On Thursday the parking lot hosts a local farmers market. Politicians come to make speeches and raise money.

The big surprise is all the surprises. There have been almost 30 weddings per year on the roof. Casual, unexpected interactions in the shared kitchen on the second floor generate new relations and new ideas. The power of social organizing around a variety of habitats and ecotones that feel safe, welcoming, and comforting is extraordinary. And it makes money, roughly 5 percent return on equity, a net of over $400,000 annually to support Ecotrust programs—not a lot in the commercial real estate world, but we have been fully leased at market rates from day one and we turn down eager potential tenants almost weekly, even during the economic bust of 2008–2009.

We tried to create a culture of listening and learning at Ecotrust, a place where experimentation and adaptation is rewarded, where failure at a new idea may be as valuable as success at an old one. We tried to create a context of what systems ecologist Buzz Holling calls "safe-fail." But a lot of the Natural Capital Center's success was dumb luck and the pace of redevelopment in the Pearl District since we opened. The Portland city streetcar stops at our corner. Kitty-corner, William Jamison Square is full of children and parents playing in the fountain on the hot days of summer—which is a good thing, because many of them enjoy Hot Lips Pizza or Laughing Planet burritos for lunch. Condominiums and retailers have replaced abandoned buildings and empty lots in the old railroad yards. There is new

The atrium, completed. It is a good watering hole.

life in the city. After all, the Jean Vollum Natural Capital Center is a living, breathing ecosystem that we hope gives new meaning to "living building," a model for urban living and—get this—a marketplace for the goods, services, and ideas of an emerging conservation economy. Jane Jacobs visited to see how we were connecting the capital, technology, and markets in the city with the supply of environmentally sound goods and services in the country. And she was proud.

DIFFERENTIATION
EMERGING FROM
GENERALITY

Jane Jacobs

We took Jane Jacobs seriously.

12

SLOW FOOD, SLOWER FORESTS

I've emphasized that we designed the Natural Capital Center based on principles found in nature. Perhaps I should have said "once found in nature," since many of the natural processes found in natural ecosystems—life processes that have evolved over thousands and millions of years—have been modified or even replaced through the ingenuity of modern technology.

Here in the Pacific Northwest, for example, we've grown almost numb to the sight of large, square clear-cuts running from river banks to the top of high ridges, enormous slash piles of butt logs, trunks, branches, and tree tops too small or of too little economic value to haul to a mill, and streams running brown with sediment from eroding soils. We still have lots of trees, but trees do not a forest make—at least not the type of forest that has evolved on the West Coast of North America over the millennia. The Northwest forest products industry quickly replaced the distinctive natural competitive advantage of this very particular forest type with "tree farms" that attempt to compete in global markets with commodity products that will always be produced at lower cost in southern and semitropical pine plantations elsewhere.

The ingenuity of modern technology has had a similar effect on the way we get our food. Just a generation ago, most Americans were still eating locally grown, relatively chemical-free food produced by small and mid-sized family farms. Today most of these small and mid-sized farms have been aggregated into relatively few large farms that rely on chemicals, machinery, and efficiency—at the expense of diverse plant communities that have not only macro but also micro nutrients that plants use to defend themselves from predation in environments free of synthetic pesticides. This approach is feeding a lot of people fast, cheap food—high-calorie, nutrient-poor food that is poisoning soil, water, air, and its customers while driving small farmers out of business and rural communities into the ground.

None of this is news. As far back as the 1980s a reporter named Carlo Petrini got caught up protesting a McDonalds opening near the Spanish Steps in Rome and helped spawn a global movement against fast-moving Western industrialized food. Since then, annual slow food conferences have grown into international events, last year attracting more than 8,000 people from most of the countries in the world, including representatives from Alaska to California. Noted agricultural essayists such as Michael Pollan have written about the destructive nature of industrial agriculture; Pollan's The Omnivore's Dilemma *and* In Defense of Food *will tell you more than you ever wanted to know about where our food comes from. Thus, what follows is merely the story of Ecotrust's fragile attempt to participate in the global slow food movement and to expand that movement to include even slower forests.*

Slow Food

It's 2005, and Eileen Brady, Ecotrust Food and Farms director, is addressing a group of farmers and chefs in a grange in Oregon's Willamette Valley, in the heart of some of the most productive farmland in the world: "Okay, now we're going to do some speed-dating. All the farmers and chefs interested in beets and root vegetables in October go to this corner; strawberries, blackberries, and Marionberries in July across the hall." There is a scraping of chairs on wood as people rise to attend their preferred appointments.

It's a simple idea: connect the supply and demand of local, seasonal food. Over several years we worked with the Portland chapter of the Chef's Collaborative, a national group representing chefs committed to fostering a sustainable food system, and helped sponsor some 20 Farmer-Chef Connection conferences from California to Washington. We invited chefs, restaurant owners, wholesalers, and grocers—along with institutional buyers like Bon Appetit Management Company, caterers, hospital food service providers, and eventually school cafeteria staff—to join for one to two days with local farmers, ranchers, and fishermen. The food producers talked about what they grew, how much they pro-

Salmon fishers of the Pacific Northwest at Slow Food's Terra Madre, Italy, 2004.

duced, and what quantities they could supply, when, how, and at what price. People exchanged business cards; new relationships grew. We produced *A Guide to Local and Seasonal Foods*, at first hard copy, then on-line.

Ultimately we wrote up a "Building Local Food Networks" toolkit, a sort of how-to beyond Farmer-Chef Connection conferences, which appears to have been helpful across the nation. It was one foot in front of the other, figuring it out as it grew, trying to iron out the problems and disagreements that inevitably arise, taking flack for not doing enough, while trying to squeeze another charitable dollar out of supporters to make it happen at all. Personalities, institutional jealousies, territorial xenophobia, understandably conservative and suspicious inclinations of farmers, and arrogant or ignorant tendencies of city folk all got in the way, but we just kept slogging along until there was something there that could be turned loose to

A Farmer-Chef Connection underway in a grange in Oregon's Willamette Valley.

positive effect. Eileen was smart, resourceful, and magnetic, and she was supported by the leadership and tenacity of Debra Sohm Lawson, who had come to Portland from a staff computing job at Conservation International.

In 2006, in collaboration with the Renewing America's Food Traditions (RAFT) Consortium, we published *Renewing Salmon Nation's Food Traditions*, edited by ethnobotanist Gary Paul Nabhan, a book describing traditional foods of our own bioregion, accompanied by a map of regional foodsheds that also ran in the *New York Times.*

In 2007, we attracted Deborah Kane from the Food Alliance, a Portland-based national organization dedicated to sustainable farm certification. Deborah was awarded a W. K. Kellogg Foundation Food & Society Policy Fellowship and continues to devote her boundless energy to Ecotrust's Food & Farms Program. She has a special interest in children and wanted to get regionally produced food into school lunches. How many kids really know where their food comes from? Studies suggest kids today are much more likely to recognize corporate logos than carrot tops growing from the soil. Clearly, there's something wrong with this picture. We have a moral obligation to help our children make healthy eating choices; they need to know what carrot tops look like.

Working with Portland Public Schools, we began with a single, small public elementary school in southeast Portland, plus a control school across the Willamette, to explore what it would take, how much it would cost, the upside and downside of farm-to-school, attitudes of students and teachers alike about different food choices. The idea was to stem the degradation and loss of family farms in the Northwest and across the country while improving children's health. The next year, our farm-to-school efforts grew to include all 80-plus schools within Portland, then a few more districts, and then across the state. Soon enough it was clear we needed to take the fight for better school food to the state capitol, where Deborah and her team led a campaign that was passed but not fund-appropriated in the legislature, and won the hearts and minds of Oregonians across the state, bringing rural and urban, Democrats and Republicans together in support of regionally grown food finding its way into the school cafeteria. Currently, we coordinate and support farm-to-school programs in eight western states, including Hawaii. Ecotrust also owns and publishes *Edible Portland*, a quarterly magazine promoting local food. And we are rolling out *FoodHub*, an online social venture effort designed to facilitate the buying and selling of local, seasonal food. Deborah likes to say that Ecotrust is building a regional food system one handshake at a time. It is about building relationships, just as Gerald Amos said.

The departments of agriculture in both Oregon and Washington are helping to fund programs here, and we like to think we're part of new Secretary of Agriculture Tom Vilsack's conversation in Washington, D.C., while we happily watch Michelle Obama plant a garden on the White House lawn. Recently, Vilsack posted a YouTube video of himself outside the USDA headquarters in downtown Washington, D.C. He began by asking: "Do you know where your food comes from?" A simple enough question, but one that has launched a new USDA campaign called "Know Your Farmer, Know Your Food." Vilsack encouraged us all to get to know some of the men and women in our area who put food on our tables each and every day: "By reconnecting consumers with local producers we will create new income opportunities for farmers, promote sustainable agricultural practices, and help generate wealth that will stay in rural communities." Vilsack concluded by saying that "today more than any other time since most Americans moved off the family farm, food and agriculture are at the center of a national conversation."

Indeed they are. And in many respects, as Deborah Kane's pioneering work suggests, the school cafeteria is ground zero of that conversation. For some kids, the meals they consume at school represent two-thirds of their total daily caloric intake on school days. So you have to ask, is the federal school meal program structured in such a way that it helps us teach children healthy eating habits? Is it structured in such a way that kids would stand a fighting chance of knowing where their food comes from? Maybe we can structure the school meal program to help our children understand that food is not a widget that comes from a far-away factory. Maybe we can teach them that food is an agricultural product that involves a jaw-dropping, awe-inspiring natural process that lets a little seed grow into a plant that produces a fruit that nourishes the body and soul. As Henry David Thoreau has it, "Convince me that you have a seed there, and I am prepared to expect wonders."

As to what seeds to plant, Thoreau went on to observe that "One is wise to cultivate the tree that bears fruit in one's soul." To which I would add that, from an economic standpoint, it is wise to cultivate the tree that bears fruit in one's bioregion.

Slower Forests

It's August 2008, and I'm standing with salmon restoration biologist Charley Dewberry in Dry Creek, a small tributary of the Sixes River on the southern Oregon coast. We're up to our knees in salmon; there must be 300 baby salmon or "fry"—coho, Chinook, and steelhead—in this single clear pool overhung by big-leaf maple, red alder, and Sitka spruce. Most are two to three inches long and shimmer red, blue, black, and even grey, beautiful when you can spot them—no easy task; their coloration was designed to camouflage them in these pools. Charley is describing what he's learned about stream ecology from more than 20 years of snorkeling streams from British Columbia to California.

"Salmon in streams like this are finding just one to two percent of the food they would have gotten 100 years ago, before logging," he says. "When you see cohort fry of the same species and same age, but of different sizes, you know there's not enough food to go around and that some are getting more food than others and growing bigger faster." Their food, he says, are stone flies, caddis, midges and other aquatic insects. And what do the insects eat? The microscopic organisms that feed off decaying leaf litter. In other words, the salmon-stream ecosystem is fed by the falling needles and leaves of the surrounding forest, particularly red alder.

Charley noticed me looking around at the forest, and added: "Yes, there are still lots of trees here, and lots of leaf litter to drive the food system that feeds salmon and, ultimately, the nutrients that the salmon supply to the ecosystem. What's different now compared to pre-logging days is stream metabolism—the way it processes organic matter." Fewer big old-growth trees fall into the stream or are driven into the streams by debris flows of rock from the steep slopes in winter storms. It was those rocks and trees cascading down steep hillsides, complete with big old-growth trees with their huge root wads, that set up debris dams that slowed stream flow and created the small pools that collected and processed organic matter. And it was in these stable pools, those held by rock and 5- to 10- to 20-foot-diameter trees that even high winter flood water couldn't budge, that most of the fry were found in the first months and years of their freshwater lives. Without the large woody material, the water washes all the food and smaller debris into the ocean in big blowout winter storms and spring floods.

Later, Charley showed me other small pools; he pointed to some rocks: "Look. These rocks don't have any moss or algae, the food base of the small aquatic insects that feed salmon fry. Look more closely and you'll see dozens of aquatic snails, eating the vegetation off the rocks. And what eats aquatic snail? Pacific giant salamanders. There are lots of snails here because I'm guessing there are few salamanders here. Why is that? Because

Charley Dewberry, salmon restoration biologist, snorkeling for stream productivity.

salamanders need large rotting logs, which aren't here because of clear-cut versus selective logging." He looked at me like a counsel for the defense about to rest his case: "Few Pacific salamanders, lots of snails, little vegetation, few aquatic insects, too little food for baby salmon, poor salmon returns, poor fishermen who can't pay mortgages on their fishing boats. What the salmon are telling us is, when we lose the natural relationships and connections in healthy ecosystems, we lose jobs."

Harry Hoogesteger, biologist, with a spawned-out chinook salmon, Dry Creek, Oregon. Healthy forest and marine ecosystems nourish tiny fry into huge, healthy, diverse, and resilent salmon populations.

And, I wanted to add, returns for forest ecosystem investors. Unfortunately, this connection between healthy ecosystems and reliable prosperity is one that we Americans are slow to learn. In 1892, Gifford Pinchot, America's first trained forester and later founder of both the Yale University Forest School and the U.S. Forest Service, began his career with the goal of developing a "regular system of forest management, the prime object of which is to pay the owner while improving the forest." Pinchot was convinced that he could "prove what America did not yet understand, that trees could be cut and the forest preserved at one and the same time." Over 100 years later, we are still a long way from understanding Pinchot's lessons.

Nowhere is this more evident than in the coastal temperate rain forests of North America, where the dominant industrial forestry model is to clear-cut and plant, a model driven by short-term "efficiencies" rather than by the very particular characteristics of the local environment, much like modern agriculture, fisheries, commercial building, and so much else we've learned from the Western reductionist model of industrial improvement. As Wendell Berry has pointed out, we once had cows living in pastures: the cows were fed, the pasture was fertilized. Then we put cows in feedlots. Now we have a fertilizer problem and a pollution problem. Instead of going back to the simple solution of cows in a pasture, we've invented two new problems. And, of course, the genius of capitalism is that these are two new opportunities to make money, but sadly, this is often what happens when technology attempts to replace nature rather than respecting and learning from it.

Take the case of the coastal temperate rain forests, that great swath of redwoods, western hemlock, Sitka spruce, Western red cedar, and Douglas fir from central California to Alaska's Kodiak Island. These forests' very particular characteristics include complexity rather than simplicity; they have a rich diversity of species, age classes, and biophysical structure. These forests have evolved over millennia in an environment of abundant rainfall throughout the year and, therefore, relative absence of summer drought and rare occurrence of catastrophic fire. The natural history of these forests is shaped principally by winter windstorms, rock and snow avalanches, changing stream courses, and individual tree fall. Because this kind of ecological disturbance, the underlying driver of ecological process is small and patchy in nature, and individual trees live long, some over 1,000 years, and grow tall and unusually large—almost 400 feet high and more than 20 feet in diameter. Nowhere in the world do forests get bigger and carry more standing biomass than coastal temperate rain forests. They store more carbon than any ecosystem on Earth. Seeds are adapted to germinate on organic seedbeds on the mossy forest floor, and trees grow slowly in the shady understory of older trees, their needles adapted to capture various levels of light. Some trees are slowly dying, creating "snags," or standing dead trees, with a variety of crevices and holes that harbor nesting insectivorous birds and arboreal mammals. Multiple canopies are supremely adapted to capturing the full range of light, moisture, and nutrients that contribute to extraordinary productivity. With diversity comes adaptation to a range of environmental stress and a resilience uncommon to simpler ecosystems. This diversity contributes as well to relatively stable, endemic populations of insects and disease, unlike the epidemic populations that often favor simpler systems driven by more catastrophic disturbance like fire.

We know all this. And yet the coastal temperate rain forests of North American have been managed by a modern industrial system that converts this distinctive diversity into monocultures and even-aged plantations of one- to 40-year-old trees. Shade-tolerant species like red cedar, which are adapted to the moist coast, have been replaced with more sun-loving Douglas fir, often genetically "improved" seedlings of a single seed source. But when we attempt to replace nature with technology, we often get surprises. One result of the industrial clear-cut and plant model on the coasts of Oregon and Washington, for example, is an increase in the incidence of Swiss needle cast, a native pathogen found at low endemic levels in natural forests, but which, in monocultures of young, even-aged Douglas fir, explodes and reduces growth or kills the trees altogether. A recent study indicates that more than 300,000 acres of Douglas fir plantations have been infected with needle cast.

Another example is red alder, a native deciduous hardwood species found on recently disturbed sites in native coastal forests. With landslides, snow avalanches, or the larger patches of disturbance created by windstorms, the light, wind-disbursed seeds of red alder quickly spread to exposed mineral soils,

212

Dry Creek, Sixes River, Oregon; an important salmon stream on Ecotrust Forests lands.

taking advantage of their unusual nitrogen-fixing ability, and grow quickly to outpace the slower-growing but longer-lived evergreen conifers. But for decades, industrial forest managers have systematically sprayed herbicides from helicopters to kill red alder and prevent it from slowing the growth of Douglas fir plantations. Recently, however, Asian log buyers discovered the excellent quality of red alder for furniture making and drove the price of red alder sawlogs to three times the value of Douglas fir saw logs. Slower-growing red cedar is also two to three times the value of the Douglas fir that has replaced it and is becoming biologically and economically extinct on many of the sites where it was historically abundant.

I could go on, but the net result of the industrial clear-cut and plant system is that it replaces the ecosystem services of diversity, productivity, resilience, and stability with expensive technological and petroleum-dependent resources that reduce the forests' distinctive characteristics. The free ecological processes that have evolved over millions of years are replaced with expensive technological systems. Where we had carbon storage, we now have burning slash piles pumping carbon-dioxide-filled smoke in the air. Where we had as much as 100,000 board feet of wood on an average acre, we now have 10,000 to 12,000 board feet per acre. Where there was flood control and soil build up, we have increased flooding, soil

Coastal temperate rain forest, Drift Creek, Oregon.

degradation, warmer water, fewer salmon-friendly and sediment-filled streams. Where there was abundant wild salmon, there are now endangered or extinct runs up and down the coast. Where there was old-growth Sitka spruce capable of building Howard Hughes' famous, if useless, six-engine Spruce Goose, the largest wood airplane in the world, there are now 10- to 18-inch-diameter Douglas fir, spruce, and western hemlock that are managed to produce only two-by-fours and pulp for toilet paper.

It was with all this in mind that, in 2005, Ecotrust created Ecotrust Forests, LLC, a for-profit private forest investment fund. Ecotrust Forests embodies the "radical" idea of going back to a centuries-old model of natural forest management, one still dominant in parts of Europe, and indeed still practiced sporadically in some of the public forests in the West, as well as in many hardwood forests back East. The capital structure of the fund is designed to match the particular nature of the forest itself—not just any forest,

Old-growth coastal temperate rain forest on Highway 101, Olympic Peninsula, Washington.

Second-growth, tree-farmed coastal rain temperate forest on Highway 101, Olympic Peninsula, Washington.

but the distinctive qualities of the coastal temperate rain forests of North America—rather than forcing the forest to serve the interests of investors looking for short-term gain.

Ecotrust Forests is the world's first ecosystem investment fund—which is to say, a fund that would restore forests while intending to pay the owners. It produces traditional forest products like saw logs for lumber and pulp logs for paper, while also producing forest ecosystem services like clean water, habitat for fish and wildlife, soil-building and carbon storage, as well as recreational opportunities. The Fund now owns 12,000 acres of highly productive second-growth forestland in coastal Oregon and Washington, four tracts upon which Ecotrust is harvesting wood, but also producing ecosystem services while restoring the natural ecosystem.

We extend the average age of rotation—the age at which trees are generally harvested—which increases the volume and quality of wood, the amount of carbon stored, and the quality of habitat

Industrial forest management, Olympic Peninsula, Washington.

Ecotrust Forest management attempts to replicate nature's model—small, patchy disturbance. Garibaldi Forest, central Oregon coast.

for native species. We restore the natural mix of species and age classes. For example, we cut more of the planted Douglas firs in order to get the species mix back to its natural diversity—Sitka spruce, red alder, and red cedar—which improves habitat. We leave snags and large trees for endangered spotted owls and nesting marbled murrelets, a diminutive sea bird that nests on the mossy limbs of large old-growth trees near the coast, and make sure that there are large conifer trees like Sitka spruce and red cedar adjacent to rivers. When they fall in, they create long-lasting pools, which are good for the fish. When we cut, we try to mimic the natural disturbances of the ecosystem—small patches usually caused by blowdowns or avalanches.

The economy of the Northwest is shifting from natural resource products to services such as tourism, hotels, restaurants, and entertainment. By layering revenues from sales of ecosystem

Nature's model of management on the Garibaldi Forest. Patch cut on the left mimics a winter wind storm blow-down on the right. December 2007.

services on top of sales of forest products, the combined long-term revenues of Ecotrust Forests are projected to be greater than traditional forest management. For example, Ecotrust Forests is selling conservation easements to protect streamside habitat and, in early 2010, closed the first substantial sale of forest carbon in the Pacific Northwest—a mechanism for capturing carbon from atmospheric CO_2 into the wood of trees. As the economy shifts from goods to services, so goes Ecotrust Forests.

Using this model—essentially, nature's model—we expect to produce competitive long-range investment returns from the full range of products and services that this forest is uniquely capable of producing, while restoring native forest characteristics and employing local people. Clearly, it's long-term rather than short-term. Ecotrust Forests is an "evergreen" fund—perpetual in duration like the forest itself, constantly taking in new investments and retiring others—rather than a fixed-term fund of 10 to 12 years like that of most timberland investment management organizations, known as "TIMOs." Ours is a "FIMO," a forestland rather than a timberland investment management organization. It's specifically designed for long-term investors interested in capital appreciation and environmental as well as social returns.

Not surprisingly, some investors have a problem with this "slow money" model. When I sent the Ecotrust Forests offering documents to Warren Buffett, the investment "Sage of Omaha," and father of one of Ecotrust's early board members, he sent the material back to me with a note: "Trees grow slow." Nevertheless, in the first two years, Ecotrust Forests attracted 35 investors willing to commit nearly $30 million to acquire and manage the land. We cut about 25 percent of annual growth by thinning individual trees and cutting small variable density patches of a few acres in size, taking out the poorer quality individuals and trying each time to improve the health, diversity, and value of the remaining forest. In the first four years of the Fund, we purchased five million board feet of merchantable volume, logged over six million board feet, and now have 102 million board feet of standing volume. In 2009, a year in which we did no logging and the forest products industry tanked, the net asset value of the Fund grew seven percent against the TIMO benchmark, which was down about five percent. Since the fund is 100 percent equity and carries no debt, we aren't forced to log to generate cash to pay interest expenses when log prices are low, as they have been from 2008 to 2010, when U.S. housing starts went from almost two million annually to fewer than 600,000 and log prices tanked. We'll let the trees grow and log some fraction of annual growth when prices are high for the particular species and logs over time. While global markets in stocks crashed in 2008–2009 by 40 percent, Ecotrust Forests' stock of trees continued to grow 7.1 percent per year.

I told Yvon Chouinard about Ecotrust Forests and was a bit startled when he invested virtually all of his 401k retirement plan. I asked if he would make public his reason to do so and his answer was vintage Chouinard: "I think the safest thing we can do is invest in what we need, not in what we want."

Looking at the forest from the perspective of the needs of salmon as well as investors is not really a new or radical idea. It's an economy that falls under the category of managing natural relations instead of "our" natural resources, an idea that indigenous people have been practicing for thousands of years. It's an economy based on gift exchange.

Clear water flowing from Ecotrust Forests Dry Creek Sixes River forest on Oregon's south coast; muddy water from clear-cut logging upstream.

13

The poet W. H. Auden once wrote, "The laws of economics . . . boil down to this: 'It is impossible to receive without giving.'" I would suggest that our current economic and environmental crises boil down to this: the industrial model of economics violates this basic law that operates in all of nature. We cannot just keep taking; we have to give back. Long-term human prosperity is simply not possible if we destroy the source from which it comes and the natural model on which it must be based. Why this advice comes from a poet rather than an economist might be the subject of another book.

The idea of gift exchange is an old one and has been part of the tension between individual and communal well-being perhaps since the human species evolved from the African savannah. Perhaps the simplest illustration of the principles involved in gift exchange is the ancient tribal ceremony in which the bones of the first salmon of each season are returned to the water to ensure that the salmon return the following year with their gift of winter food. But not all of the examples are ancient.

The Lost Totem Pole

In 1993, at the height of our negotiations in the Kitlope, Cecil Paul was searching for something that had been taken many

221

Cecil Paul telling the story of the Na na kila pole, Kemano Village site, British Columbia.

years before. *G'psgolox* was the name of a totem pole once com-
missioned by the village chief of the now-abandoned village of
Miskusa, at the mouth of the Kitlope River overlooking the estuary, to help keep the spirits of the epidemics away and render
his remaining people safe. It had been handed down over the
generations and formally belonged to Dan Paul, Cecil's brother,
but no one knew who had taken it and where it might be.

It was the dawn of the Internet that allowed friends of Cecil
to track down the pole to the Folk Museum in Stockholm, where
it had stood for almost a century. They learned that *G'psgolox*
had been taken in the early part of the century by the Swedish
consul, who wanted to bring something of his experience in
British Columbia home. Locating it was just half the battle
however. Cecil, his sister Louisa, and Gerald Amos traveled to
Stockholm to find their long-lost pole and negotiate its return.
There they found an affable museum director named Per Bak,

who listened carefully to their case. They asked to see the pole, adorned themselves in traditional button blankets, and had an emotional reunion with *G'psgolox*.

Over the course of several visits with the Haisla, the museum director was clearly sympathetic, but expressed his own responsibility to care for the pole. He was conscious of the implications of repatriating an important indigenous artifact—not only for his own museum, but also for the many around the world faced with similar demands. Never had a Canadian First Nation totem pole been returned to its original owners. Gerald offered a deal: we'll build you an identical replacement pole and we can make an exchange. The museum director said that was fair, but that the original pole would have to be kept in museum conditions to continue its care. The Haisla explained that was not the way they honored their totems, which would stand proud

Cecil Paul, seated left, with his brother Dan, seated third from left, owner of the *G'psgolox* pole, their sister Louisa, seated right, with Haisla family and elders upon return of the pole.

Arrival of the replacement *G'psgolox* pole at the Henaakisiala village site of Miskusa, at the mouth of the Kitlope River, July 2005.

where they were originally built and eventually return to the earth from whence they came. Gerald then offered to build a second replacement pole that would be raised at the original site at Miskusa, and they would build a museum in Kitamaat for the ultimate care of the original *G'psgolox*. It was a long and emotional negotiation, and the Haisla in fact had no resources with which to build another pole, to say nothing of two poles plus a museum in Kitamaat Village.

But Gerald, Louisa, and Cecil are nothing if not persuasive. With no formal education other than his brief time at the residency school in Nanaimo, Cecil is the most articulate man I've ever met. He got going after dinner one evening on a fundraising trip I had organized on a restored mission boat with Jean Vollum and David Rockefeller Jr. and did a monologue until almost midnight that kept his audience alternatively spellbound and in tears. For his part, Gerald is a virtuoso diplomat—at once clear, smart, and infinitely reasonable. And Cecil's sister Louisa is resolute, with a very strong sense of identity, persistence, and justice. Their collective logic and humanity is irrefutable.

By this time in 1995, we had started Ecotrust Canada to bring additional resources and Canadian sensibilities to play in British Columbia. Ian Gill, the Australian reporter who wrote for *The Vancouver Sun* and later did evening news and documentaries for CBC Television, had followed the Kitlope story while also covering the evolving battleground over another of Canada's last great temperate rain forests in Clayoquot Sound on Vancouver Island. Ian was with us on Kitlope Lake with Gerald, Cecil, and Louisa, along with John Cashore and ministry officials, when I asked him if he knew anyone who might be a good executive director for Ecotrust Canada. Eventually he took the bait and did a terrific job growing Ecotrust Canada from a Vancouver base. Ian supported Gerald and the Haisla on the return of the

Haisla chief Kenny Hall welcoming Sami reindeer-herding representatives from Sweden.

225

G'psgolox replacement pole at the old Miskusa village site at the mouth of the Kitlope River.

pole, raising hundreds of thousands of dollars for the project. He helped get two red cedar logs donated for the replacement poles; arranged for Overwaitea, the grocery chain, to ship the poles to Vancouver, where Boeing agreed to put them on board a brand new 747 being delivered to SAS, Scandinavian Airline; and arranged for a National Film Board documentary team to film the whole project over the course of almost a decade.

So in the summer of 2005, the Haisla people hosted a celebration at Miskusa to mark the raising of Dan Paul's *G'psgolox* replacement pole. Hundreds of people came from all over the world: representatives of the Folk Museum, the grand chief of Canada's Assembly of First Nations, two Sami people, the reindeer-herding indigenous people of Sweden, artists, Haisla people, representatives of Greenpeace Europe, the Ford Foundation from New York, Peter and Jennifer Buffett, Ecotrust and Ecotrust Canada representatives, the Royal Canadian Mounted Police, and—a big surprise—the granddaughter of the Swedish consul who had taken the pole to Sweden, a woman in her seventies, along with her daughter. The weather was dreadful—fog, rain, and low clouds. People had to come 80 kilometers from Kitamaat Village by boat and floatplanes. The pole and guests had to come into the old village site on a high tide, then leave on another high tide and get back to Kitamaat before dark. There were old people, chiefs and elders, and babies. And the film crew with their equipment. There were meals to prepare, welcoming ceremonies and speeches, songs and drumming. Plus the whole crowd had to do something that hadn't been done for perhaps 200 years: erect a 30-foot tall, two-ton totem pole. No one knew how. But the artists built a cement foundation and a large steel hinge, and we brought along rope. Lots of rope. Today, *G'psgolox* stands proud in its new home.

Original *G'psgolox* pole lying in state back home in Kitamaat Village. Carver Henry Robertson seated.

I tell this story not only as a modern example of gift exchange with a twist, but also as an illustration of the ingenuity, resourcefulness, and tenacity of indigenous leaders. How Ecotrust eventually decided to reward, encourage, and support such leadership is yet another story.

The Ecotrust Indigenous Leadership Award

Jack Vaughn called me one day shortly after we started Ecotrust. Jack was our founding chair and served for nine years, the maximum allowed. "Spencer, I think I'm going to finally bring home the bacon," he said. "I serve on the board of the Pan American Development Foundation. Howard Buffett serves with me. He told me he wants to be on the board of an environmental organization with a global perspective and a human face. I told him about Ecotrust. You should call him." I did, and Howard said yes.

Howard Buffett took his responsibilities seriously. He wanted to get into the field and get to know the rain forests of home. And photograph bears; he was big on charismatic megafauna. We flew to Juneau, then to Admiralty Island when the salmon were spawning, and I did the staff-board thing: held an umbrella over his head in the pouring rain while he photographed grizzlies feeding in a stream. We also went to the Kitlope with Gerald Amos and to Kodiak Island, Alaska.

One day in 1999, Howard grew tired of me carrying on about the extraordinary leadership capacities and stories of survival and determination among Native American and First Nations people like Gerald Amos and Cecil Paul: "Why don't you do an annual award and recognize these people?" he said. "Something simple and straightforward. Just help them tell the world what they've done. I'll give you $25,000 a year plus some funding to administer it. Write it up. Maybe my brother Peter will do something too."

"Good idea, Howard," I said. *Why didn't I think of that?* I muttered to myself. And Peter and his wife, Jennifer, did join in. Sons of Warren Buffett, both Howard and Peter, and their families led relatively simple lives. Howard and his wife, Devon, lived in Decatur, Illinois. He liked nothing better than working on his small corn farm. He served on some agricultural business boards, was an avid photographer, and published a series of books. Peter Buffett was a musician and lived in a modest old residential neighborhood in Milwaukee. Peter produced a series of musicals called *Spirit*, honoring the stories of Native American song, dance, and stories. He also wrote the score for Kevin Costner's film "Dances with Wolves."

Peter gets it. Howard gets it. One of the glorious things they did in a quiet and unassuming way was fund the repatriation of 120 acres of land at the mouth of the Koeye River in Heiltsuk and Oweekeno First Nation Territory, near Bella Bella, British Columbia. It was one of the watersheds in British Columbia over 50,000 acres in size that remained intact, except for a small piece at the mouth of the river that had been patented from public to private ownership, logged, then resold to an enterprising individual in Vancouver who

built a Quality-Inn-style lodge and planned commercial sport fishing and hunting. But Koeye was Heiltsuk-Owekeeno territory, traditional home to Ed Newman, a hereditary chief of the Heiltsuk and a tough character with no particular love of white people. With Howard and Peter's help we bought the lodge and surrounding land and gave it back free and clear, as it should have been, to the people who had called it home for thousands of years and defended it from additional industrial logging and development.

The Koeye bears on the story of indigenous leadership of people like Ed Newman, but also on the extraordinary things that

Guujaaw at the Ecotrust Indigenous Leadership Award ceremony, 2006.

229

W. Ron Allen, Jamestown S'Kallam Tribe, at Ecotrust Indigenous Leadership Award ceremony.

can be done by gentle philanthropists like the Buffetts. And it bears on the idea of gift exchange, the reciprocal process made poignant by an unusual incident at the ceremony on the beach at the Koeye the summer of 2001. Over 200 guests were arriving. Elder Heiltsuk women were weaving cedar baskets with children and friends. People were setting up tents, preparing food, and getting ready for a big bonfire and feast in the evening. Liz Woody, a Warm Springs–Navajo woman who managed the leadership awards program for Ecotrust, and her friend Dave Hatch, a Siletz Oregon tribal member from Portland, had just stepped off a fishing boat from Bella Bella. Coho salmon were running and young Heiltsuk tribal members were fishing along the sandy

230

beach. At one point, one of them flung a salmon 30 feet into the sand. I thought that an odd way to treat fresh salmon for the feast, until I saw a bald eagle which had been watching from a tall spruce nearby swoop down and pick up the fish, one of several provided by the young Heiltsuk. Liz and Dave had the big surprise when a salmon fell out of the sky in front of their feet as they walked down the beach; they looked up and saw an eagle fly by—yet another gift exchanged, apparently. They cleaned the salmon and prepared it for the celebration.

The Buffetts created what we first called the Buffett Award for Indigenous Leadership, but, as the Buffetts didn't want to call attention to themselves, later it was changed to the Ecotrust Indigenous Leadership Award. The award recognizes individual leaders who are enrolled members of their native tribe working to improve environmental, social, and/or economic well-being in the salmon bioregion from Alaska to California. It recognizes leaders who have made extraordinary contributions to their people and surrounding communities and are examples of strength, wisdom, and perseverance to society at large. Written nominations are accepted throughout the year and read by a panel of Native and First Nations members, Ecotrust, Ecotrust Canada, ShoreBank board and staff, and citizens of the region. The reading panel chooses five finalists and forwards these to a jury of five distinguished indigenous leaders, who then choose an awardee. All five individuals, their families, and guests are invited to an annual dinner at the Jean Vollum Natural Capital Center. The winner receives $25,000, with which they can do as they wish, and the other four finalists each receive $5,000. We publicize their achievements, and do what we can to support their work.

In 2003, the Buffett brothers endowed the award with a $500,000 gift to Ecotrust's Natural Capital Fund, so we are hopeful that the process of recognition will continue indefinitely, and the growing number of finalists will be a naturally expanding network that assumes increasing responsibility for the governance of the program. By 2009, the network consisted of 39 finalists. By 2022 there should be a network of almost 100 remarkable leaders who help guide Ecotrust and Ecotrust Canada's work and whose stories inspire initiative both here and around the world.

The first awardee was Phillip Cash Cash, a Nez Perce–Cayuse linguist enrolled in the Confederated Tribes of Umatilla Indians in Northeast Oregon. Phillip is earning a PhD from the University of Arizona and has devoted his career to restoring and teaching the Nez Perce language. The jury felt that the loss of language was a loss of the cultural understanding of thousands of years of continuous occupation, a loss equivalent to the loss of genetic information captured in the full range of biodiversity.

Successive awardees have included Clarence Alexander, a hereditary and elected leader of the Gwich'in peoples, whose life was devoted to keeping the Yukon River potable, a powerful counterpoint to oil and gas development on the nearby North Slopes of Alaska; Guujaaw, the Haida leader who has worked with his community on Haida Gwaii, a group of islands off the coast of British Columbia, to repatriate control of management of their lands and customs; Billy Frank Jr., a Puyallup tribal member near Olympia, Washington, who has devoted his lifetime to fighting for treaty rights and the restoration of salmon in the Northwest. Tawna Sanchez was recognized for her work with abused native children in urban environments; Bob Sam, a T'lingit from Sitka, Alaska, for his stories; Teri Rofgar, also T'lingit, for her craft. W. Ron Allen, elected chief of the Jamestown Clallam on the Olympic Peninsula, Washington, helped rebuild his tribe from a handful of enrolled members to thousands, raised millions for business development, health care and educational facili-ties, and serves on regional and national boards pursuing Native American interests. Robert used his $25,000 as a down payment on a national tribal effort to build an American Indian Embassy in Washington, D.C. It opened in the fall of 2009. Jeanette Armstrong, representative of the Oka'nagon people in the upper Columbia River Basin of British Columbia, was recognized for her work with tribal land restoration and education.

All of these people have used their awards to continue their work. They come to the awards ceremony with their families and tribal representatives, who they in turn recognize as the source of their own success. They do not act as individuals and generally eschew any sense of authority or ownership. Their leadership gifts are made possible only by the power of their relationships. Each of the honorees for the Ecotrust Indigenous Leadership Award represent remarkable achievements in their own right and are resourceful in ways unimaginable to most people today. But they also bring a spirit of community, a sharing attitude that is their own way of pursuing a more reliable prosperity.

The real heroes of this book are the people I've met along the way, and from whom I've learned much. The recipients of the Ecotrust Indigenous Leadership Awards are high on my list of heroes. What I've learned from them is that culture is more powerful than money and technology, and that values trump politics. Societies indeed do what societies think, and what we think is shaped by the places we love and by the stories of those places. William Kittredge, a writer who grew up on a ranch in southeastern Oregon, puts it well: "We live in stories. What we *are* is stories. We do things because of what is called character, and our character is formed by the stories we learn to live in."

Such stories are the true source of wealth. You might call them our "cache."

2006 Ecotrust Indigenous Leadership Award honorees at the Portland Art Musuem.

Epilogue

It's said about the great physicist Neils Bohr that, brilliant as he was, he could not grasp the simple concept of beginnings, middles, and ends. An essay that Bohr wrote as a child in grade school has been preserved. The last sentence reads: "And I would also like to mention aluminum."

Though my editor might disagree, I do understand that a story is supposed to have a beginning, middle, and end, but the bigger story I'm telling here has no end, just further understanding that people are part of nature. In the preceding stories I've focused—or at least tried to—on the idea that our prosperity, if it is to be reliable, must be grounded in processes that operate in the rest of the natural world. In practice, this entails careful observation and sound science, but it also means trusting our instincts. It means innovation, adaptation, evolution. It means understanding that new technologies arise from old ones, or combinations of old ones, which in turn drive economic development and new science, not the other way around. It means learning as we go, reaching sometimes backward to what we thought we knew, sometimes forward to what we don't yet know.

For example, I have no idea what the fate of ShoreBank might be or where the slow food or slower forests movements will go next. But why stop with food and forests? Why not a slow fisheries movement that might start with wild versus farmed salmon? Slow money and more community banking. Slow "living building" and slow energy movements? Imagine the power when all these movements begin to connect.

Networks of networks of local initiative, jujitsuing the power of the underlying forces of globalization to the advantage of the local, the true democratization of money, technology, and information—this is the core of a more resilient development model for reliable prosperity. At Ecotrust, we call this "Salmon Nation."

Leading citizens of Salmon Nation gather on the roof of the Natural Capital Center: left to right: Anthony Boutard, farmer; Gun Denhart, business and civic leader; Yvon Chouinard; Marc Chord, logger; the author; Oregon Governor John Kitzhaber; Gloria Brown, Siuslaw National Forest Supervisor; Laura Anderson, fisherwoman; Peter Kirby, Tlingit native leader; Cameron Healy, businessman and philanthropist; and Antone Minthorn, Chairman of the Confederated Tribes of Umatilla Indians.

Salmon Nation

I'm constantly reminded of what Dave Foreman, the founder of Earth First, said to a college student who asked what is the single most important thing she could do for the environment: "Stay home!"

But what is "home?" What are its critical characteristics? What are the concentric circles of social, environmental, and economic relationships that sustain us at home? And how do we leave home a little better than we found it?

In my home, the greater Pacific Northwest, the distinctive environmental conditions—the natural flows of energy and most powerful networks of relationships that connect us—aren't hard to determine. This is the place where wild Pacific salmon live. That means this "home," if we follow the fish, is the whole north Pacific, including parts of China, the Russian far east, Japan, Alaska, British Columbia, Washington, Oregon, and California; the Pacific Ocean north of roughly a 14 degree isotherm to the Arctic. This is a place defined by abundant water, by coastlines and estuaries and mountains and forests, by streams and rivers and lakes, by grasslands and high desert—a rich biodiversity and a 10,000- to 15,000-year history of supporting relatively dense populations of hunter-gatherer people with extraordinary art and culture and mythologies of place. On its eastern shores are found the largest temperate rain forests of the world from the redwoods of California to the hemlock, spruce, cedar, and fir of southeast Alaska.

But, as Jim Lichatowich has said, places are defined as much by events as by geography. And, again, the event that has defined this place, for thousands and thousands of years, is the return of the salmon—millions and millions and millions of salmon. Though today the defining event may be a trip to the mall, for millennia, people and salmon coevolved here in the streams that followed the last glacial retreat, together with the forests and grasslands that developed in the glacial till. Salmon connect us. When salmon decline, it tells us that our farming, our fishing, our forestry, our road building, transportation and energy systems, and cities are eroding ecosystems. When 20,000 to 30,000 healthy fall Chinook salmon die within days of entering the Klamath River, as they did in 2006 due to excessively low water flows from agricultural diversion, we know our governance, our economy, our politics are failing. Politicians may deny this, but salmon don't lie.

And this is why we at Ecotrust call the greater North Pacific bioregion "Salmon Nation." Which raises certain questions. Are nature states as important an organizing and governing principle as nation states? Are all the people who live in Salmon Nation its

Salmon Nation covers five percent of Earth's surface.

citizens? Do they not then have responsibilities as well as rights to make it a better place? Who will write its declaration of inter-dependence and organize its constitutional assembly? Where is its flag, its passport? Where are its leaders, what is expected of its citizens, by what rules should we play? What goods and services does it produce better than the next best place, and for whom? What institutions and institutional arrangements help its citizens to prosper reliably? What will be its stories, its myths? To what spirits do we pray? What do the people who prospered here for such a long, long time tell us about how to live well and honorably in this place? Salmon Nation. It's just one of many hopeful ideas.

I hope it's clear by now that "reliable prosperity" doesn't mean getting rich quick or, in the narrowest sense of the word, even getting "rich" at all. Reliable prosperity implies a sense of deep security, independence, and self-sufficiency. It means people having choices about where they live, what kind of work they do, a sense of self-confidence about being able to get what they need,

238

if not always everything they want. It means a certain resilience; an ability to save enough to get through rough patches the way ecosystems store energy in good times of growth and enough reserves to rebuild after major disturbances such as storms or fire or drought. It means diverse, functioning ecosystems and diverse job opportunities. It is resilient if unpredictable.

At the launch of a big international conference in Australia many years ago about a world conservation strategy, an aboriginal woman spoke. She said, "If you have come here to save me, you can go home now. But if you see my struggle as part of your own survival, maybe—maybe—we can work together."

My struggle is to put flesh on the bones of a bioregional narrative, the story of Salmon Nation, that might be applicable worldwide. Wherever you call home, I would encourage you to do likewise, since we are all part of a common struggle not only to survive, but to thrive. I suggest that we spend less time tweaking

Citizens of Salmon Nation celebrate at the Natural Capital Center, 2007.

the existing political-industrial system, and organize our work around our homes—to build something smarter, cheaper, and more equitable. A new and intimate co-evolution of people and place—what our friend Cecil Paul calls "building a magic canoe," a metaphorical one that gets bigger as more people join in the journey. For it is only by focusing our energy on the importance of place—of working with local communities, businesses, and cultures to preserve the distinctive qualities that need to be protected and restored, of releasing the energy of local residents— that we can build on the local differences that are the very foundation of human prosperity.

I'd mention aluminum except that I'm not particularly interested in aluminum—at least not at the moment. But I'm not ruling it out.

Acknowledgments

Gary Miranda, our editor, colleague, and friend, showed remarkable patience and understanding as we struggled through these stories. Without his ability to sit down at the computer and work through the night, this book might have never seen the light of day.

Jane Jacobs was the inspiration for this book, and I hope she would approve.

James Lavadour tolerated frequent interruptions in our quest to understand the depth of his profound intelligence and artistic ability.

Ofelia Svart is my longtime assistant and, for reasons unknowable, has to this day persisted through our journey from The Nature Conservancy International, to Conservation International, to Ecotrust.

My son Sam and I have had the good fortune of generous support from a number of friends and donors that allowed us the time and travel that made *Cache* possible: former Ecotrust Chairmen Bob Friedman and Cameron Healy, John and Kirsten Swift, Tim and Karen Hixon, Sophie Craighead and the Charles Engelhard Foundation, Gilman Ordway, Bill and Sally Neukom, and Nancy Schaub.

The list of people to whom I am deeply grateful might fill another book. Apologies to the many I may have overlooked. We are indebted to Christy Walton for her generous hospitality, as well as to Beatríce Aviles Verdugo and Armída Verdugo Aviles. Dave Morine, Jon Roush, Pat Noonan, and Bob Jenkins—yes, he of the "element occurrences"—were all sources of inspiration in the early days of The Nature Conservancy. To Ken Margolis, from whom I learned most everything and whose loyalty over almost 40 years is, for reasons I don't fully understand, unflagging. To Sam Diack and Franny Diack for sharing stories of their family in the early days of The Nature Conservancy. To Tom McAllister and his grandson Tristan McAllister for their help recalling and documenting our work together on the Sandy River and Sycan Marsh. To Dan Vollum for his friendship and support over the years, and of course to his mother Jean and the whole Vollum family for their generous support of our many crazy adventures together. Through his own persistence and dedication, Guy Bonnivier helped my Uncle Gordon Beebe and himself leave a legacy of precious spring creeks restored to their former glory. Bud Purdy kindly shared his thoughts about Silver Creek as a neighbor, donor, and farmer. To Alice and Kenny Gleason, who built the Circle 8 ranch from scratch, provided a constant source of the warmest kind of hospitality, and were godparents to Janie's and my dear daughter Lydia. To Al and Sally Haas, Lee and Ginny Bargaugh, and Jim Culver for their roles in caring for the Circle 8, their guests, and the Rocky Mountain Front. To Cathy MacDonald and Craig Benz at The Nature Conservancy's Oregon Office for their help in learning the results of our work on Sycan Marsh. Dick Mecham kindly helped bring the ZX Ranch perspective to the Sycan story. And to Hawk Hyde, wherever he might be riding these days.

Martin Goebel was a colleague at The Nature Conservancy International, a founder of Conservation International, and helped get some of the facts right on our stories about conservation in Mexico. Tim Means continues our long friendship and support and fights constantly for a sensible mix of conservation and business in the Sea of Cortez, along with his colleague and our friend Alejandro Robles. Helmut Janka's long search for an effective model of development in Mexico has been a source of encouragement. Dr Jose Sarúkhan and Andres Marcelo Sada were extraordinary stalwarts of good sense, generosity, and wise counsel in the early days of our work together in Mexico and in the creation of Conservation International. To Alvaro Ugalde and his many colleagues, who have created a model national system of conservation admired the world over. Among Alvaro's colleagues, to Rodrigo Gamez, Mario Boza, Liliana Madrigal, Pedro Leon, Luis Diego Gomez, as well as the maestro of meddling Dan Janzen and his wife Winnie Wallechs, who will one day properly be a made a saint. Mario Baudin, Carmen Miranda, Jorge Añez Claros, Herbert Trapu, Juan Carlos Miranda and Marcelo helped make a revisit to Bolivia productive. A special thanks to all 50+ founders of Conservation International, people like Guillermo Mann and Ernesto Barriga Bonilla, but particularly the Latin American women on the staff like Soledad Gompf, Maria Ortiz Thompson, Raquel Gomez, and many others who brought the emotional and revolutionary spirit that made it happen. And to Carol James, my early and loyal assistant there. And to Guido Rahr III, who rode through The Nature Conservancy International and Conservation International and now runs the Wild Salmon Center in Portland. To an anonymous donor who put gas in our tank many times; I would have been wildly steering a parked car for almost 40 years without her. And to Peter Seligmann and Russ Mittermeier for making CI into something substantial. Jack Vaughn has been a source of inspiration for 40 years; without him there might have been no Conservation International or Ecotrust. And to our other founding board members at CI, especially Chuck and Helen Marie Hedlund and Peter Stroh. Paul Hawken stepped in at a critical, fragile moment in CI's early history and helped us find the way forward. Gerald Amos will always be a friend and counselor; Cecil Paul a spiritual leader with wider influence than he might have anticipated. Bruce Hill was an unsung hero of the Kitlope and continues to heft a mighty spear. Dave Nisbet, Mugs Petit, and Dick and Jan Wilson helped me dredge up some of our memories of the early days in Willapa Bay. Doug and Kris Tompkins are an inspiration to the world and generously shared their homes and their work in Chile on several occasions. Their pilot Rodrigo Noriega helped make getting around in big wild country in Chile look easy. To George Patterson for his sense of adventure, good humor, hospitality, and fountain of originality. Dorothy Baert and Peter Buckland helped on a revisit to Clayoquot Sound. Rick Steiner and RJ Kopchak were the gadflies who got things off the ground in Prince William Sound and the Copper River. RJ and his wife Barkley put Sam and me up unexpectedly for a week when we were weathered in at Cordova. Bill Webber helped Sam and me explore some of the ways in which Jane Jacobs's ideas become a reality on the ground. Paul Benoit is an Obama-style community organizer and has made all kinds of good things happen in Astoria and helped create the story of the Mill Pond restoration reflect a closer reality. Ron Grzywinski, Mary Houghton, John Berdes, Mike Dickerson, John Haines, and Dave Williams made it all happen at ShoreBank. Both Ron and Mary were loyal, tenacious board members at Ecotrust, and Ron continues today at both Ecotrust and Ecotrust Canada despite the enormous challenges of keeping the remarkable legacy of ShoreBank alive and well. Yvon Chouinard and his wife, Malinda, are true north and have had a positive influence on both Sam and me in more ways than they will ever know. Howard and Peter Buffett made some important things endure. Charley Dewberry explains stream dynamics better than anyone I know. And John Gordon and Jerry Franklin likewise in the forest.

The list of colleagues at Ecotrust is yet another book and there will be many former and current staff, board members, donors, and colleagues who are simply too numerous to list. Jack Vaughn, once again, our founding board chair and pugnacious leading light. Bob Friedman and Cameron Healy were mentioned for their generous financial support of *Cache* but served many long years on the board and as board chairs, wise counsel, and generous supporters then and now. Gun Denhart, our vital new chair, quickly discovered that Ecotrust is a participatory sport, on our first adventure together in the Kitlope. Arthur Dye, Bettina von Hagen, Alana Probst, Ted Wolf, and as much as anyone else, Ed Backus were early critical staff at Ecotrust; Ed, Ken Margolis, and Ofelia Svart have come the whole wild ride from The Nature Conservancy International, Conservation International, and Ecotrust. Adam Lane, Howard Silverman, Seth Walker, Nancy Bales, Elizabeth Woody, Craig Jacobson, Deborah Kane, and Andrew Fuller have all played roles in the production of *Cache*. Stewart Brand, longtime Ecotrust Advisory Council member, was a vital spark in putting the Natural Capital Center on track. Our thanks to Ian Gill for his companionship working together with Ecotrust Canada for 15 years and his keen editorial eye on early drafts, and good wishes now as he launches Ecotrust Australia. Frederick Reimers helped with some editing as well, and Sarah Malarkey at Chronicle Books kindly offered her advice about publishing. Ross Eberman at Carpe Diem Books finally brought it all together in published form, collaborating with the creative talent of Ian Shimkoviak and Alan Hebel of The Book Designers, and the production expertise of Dick Owsiany.

Finally, none of this would have happened without my loving wife, Janie, to whom *Cache* is dedicated, or indeed without our three remarkable children, Silas, Sam, and Lydia.

Photo Credits

All photographs by Sam Beebe and Spencer B. Beebe except as noted:

Page 3, *Blue Basalt* by James Lavadour
Page 8, Robert Livingstone Beebe
Page 9 top, Hugh L. H. Dick
Page 10, Alfred Corbett
Page 23, The Nature Conservancy
Page 38, Al Haas
Page 40, Donny Kerr
Page 46, © Mark Hedrick/The Nature Conservancy
Page 48, © Craig Bienz/The Nature Conservancy
Page 110, Jane Beebe
Page 115, John Kelson
Page 136, Martin Bloom
Page 163, Adrian Dorst
Page 165, David Thomson
Page 183, ShoreBank Pacific
Page 189, unknown
Page 190 top, unknown
Page 191, Will Roush
Page 193, used by permission © SkyShots, Portland, OR
Page 194, Walsh Construction/Ecotrust
Pages 196-197, Melissa Tatge/Ecotrust
Page 204, Debra Sohm Lawson/Ecotrust
Page 209, Charley Dewberry
Page 210, courtesy of Harry Hoogesteger
Page 233, Andrew Fuller
Page 238, Analisa Gunnel/Ecotrust

Cover painting, *Cache,* by James Lavadour.

Index

Note: Bolded page numbers indicate photographs and their captions.

A

Academia de Ciencias Nacional de Bolivia, 62, 84–85, 88
Ahousaht First Nations people, 160
Alexander, Clarence, 232
Allen, W. Ron, **230**, 232
Amazon basin, 82, **83**
Amos, Gerald, 118–119, 124, **126**, 127, **128**, 132–133, 222–225
Anderson, Robert, 46
Arce, Elena Ulate, 67–68, **68**
Arctic National Wildlife Refuge, 170–171
Armstrong, Jeanette, 232
Astoria, Oregon, 173–174, 180–181

B

Backus, Edward, 167
Bahía de Ascención, Cancun, 56
Baird, Spencer Fullerton, 7
Baja Expeditions, La Paz, 58
Bak, Per, 222–223
Banco Nacional de Bolivia, 84–85
Bank of Astoria, 174, 181
Barnard, Geoff, 76
Barrs, Carrington E., 195
Beebe, Charles Francis, 8, 136–137
Beebe, Janie Magavern, 1, 49, 105–110, **109**
Beebe, Sam, 132, 143
Beebe, Spencer B., **6**, **8**, **9**, **23**, **38**, **110**, **126**, **136**
    background, 7–10
    childhood of, 14, 96
    marriage and honeymoon voyage, 107–110
    Peace Corps experience, 53–54, 99–104
    resignation from The Nature Conservancy, 13–14, 30, 78–79, 113
Beebe Company, 8, 137
Beinz, Craig, 48
Benoit, Paul, **173**, 173–174, 180–181
Berdes, John, 174, 181–183
Berry, Wendell, 211
Biddle, Nicholas, 7
Biddle, Spencer, 7, 22
Bill and Melinda Gates Foundation, 183
Bill Healy Foundation, 196
Billy Frank Jr. Conference Center, 197

Blair, Bill, 73–74
Bob Marshall Wilderness Area, 32, 36–37
Boise Cascade, 26–27
Bolivia
    Beni, 60–63
    Beni River, 82–84, 88
    bottom-up approach in, 82
    debt-for-nature swaps in, 86–87
    El Porvenir ranch, 61–62, **62**, 63–64, 84–85, 87–89, **89**, **90**
Bonnivier, Guy, **23**, 27–28, **29**
Boren, Ashley, 76–77
Boren, Frank, 73, 75–77
Boutard, Anthony, **236**
BP oil spill, Gulf of Mexico, 167
Brady, Eileen, 203, 205
Brand, Stewart, 186, 191–192
British Columbia
    Kitamaat Village, 118, 125, 224
    Ministry of Forests, 122, 125
    Tofino, 155–156, 160
    tree farm licenses, 120, 160–161
    See also Clayoquot Sound, British Columbia; Kitlope watershed, British Columbia
British Crown, 120, 155–156, 160–161
Brown, Gloria, 232
brownfield redevelopment, 173–174, 180–181
Buffett, Devon, 228–229
Buffett, Howard, 228–231
Buffett, Jennifer, 228
Buffett, Peter, 228–231
Bumble (golden retriever), 187
Burrell, Peter, 38, **38**, 39

C

cache, 1, 4, 233
Cache (Lavadour), 1
capitalism, creative, 185
Cash Cash, Phillip, 232
Cashore, John, 125, **126**, 127, 225
Castri, Francesco di, 157
Castroviejo, Javier, 60–61
cattle
    grazing by, 27–28, 43, 46–47, 63–64
    ranchers and, 34–35, 40–41, 88
Centros de Datos para la Conservacion (CDC), 66–67, 69
Chef's Collaborative, 203–204